ERASING OFFENSE

DEFEATING THE ENEMY'S SCHEME TO DESTROY YOUR RELATIONSHIPS

DUANE SHERIFF

Published by Harrison House Publishers
Shippensburg, PA 17257

ISBN 13 TP: 978-1-6675-0251-9
ISBN 13 eBook: 978-1-6675-0252-6

For Worldwide Distribution, Printed in the U.S.A.
1 2 3 4 5 6 7 8 / 27 26 25 24 23

CONTENTS

INTRODUCTION

*If you abide in my word, you are my
disciples indeed. And you shall know the
truth, and the truth shall make you free.*
—JOHN 8:31–32 NKJV

Learning to deal with and process offense has had a profound effect on my life, home, and ministry. Unfortunately, most people have not learned this valuable lesson.
They engage in offense having no idea the damage it creates in the human heart and life. Some don't even realize
they are offended! As a pastor, I often find myself explaining to people that most of the problems they experience in their marriage, in their family, or on the job are a
result of offense. This shocks them, yet scripture says our
enemy comes to steal, kill, and destroy (see John 10:10).
He does not want us happily married or at peace with

our children. He doesn't want our churches united. And he certainly doesn't want peace within our government.

Offense is one of Satan's greatest weapons. It's the root cause of marital collapse and family rifts. It's the reason politics have become so volatile. It's also why many believers remain immature and churches spiral into dysfunction.

Satan thrives on division, strife, contention, and offense. He uses offense to steal the Word of God from our hearts and create chaos in our lives. Even ministers fall into his trap. Offense amongst church leaders and staff creates a "staff infection" that hinders the move and power of God by opening the door to envy, strife, and *"every evil work"* (James 3:16).

The dangers of offense are far-reaching—offense steals our peace, destroys relationships, and can ultimately warp our personalities—yet most people have not been taught how to process it. Thankfully, the Word of God gives us the tools we need to recognize, process, and avoid offense. Psalm 119:165 says, *"Great peace have they which love thy law: and nothing shall offend them."*

You'd probably be hard-pressed to find someone in your circle of influence who does not get offended. But the Bible says, if we truly love God's Word and embrace its teaching, we'll have great peace. Not just peace, but great peace. Nothing will be able to offend us. Imagine that. Imagine living at peace with your spouse. At peace with your children. Imagine having peace in your workplace. Peace in your school and with other believers. Dear ones, it is possible.

I have lived at peace with those in my circle of relationships for decades. Since God has made peace with me through the blood of His cross, I can live at peace, not only with God, but with my fellow man. I can live in peace with my wife and children. I can have peace in my church, peace with my staff. I don't have to live in strife. I don't have to be jealous of other ministry gifts. I don't have to feel uncomfortable around those who've wronged me. How? It starts by loving God's Word (see Psalm 119:165).

None of us—from the least to the greatest—is immune to the temptation of offense. You'll probably have opportunity to get offended just reading this book! But we don't have to live in offense. If we understand the deadliness of offense and learn to recognize how Satan uses it to steal the fruit of our righteousness, we will find it easier to deal with and overcome offense in our lives.

In this book, I'll show you how. I'll define offense and reveal its long-term effects using both biblical and personal examples. I'll teach you how to discern offense in general and identify the offenses in your own life. I'll show you how to process offense and take the necessary steps to overcome it so you can reverse its effects in your life and family. With time, as you abide in and love God's Word, these truths will set you free.

CHAPTER ONE

THE DANGER OF OFFENSE

---

*An offended friend is harder to win back
than a fortified city. Arguments separate
friends like a gate locked with bars.*
—PROVERBS 18:19 NLT

Offense is one of the most dangerous heart conditions in our society, affecting believers and nonbelievers alike. But offense may not be what you think.

All of us face opportunities to become offended. Understanding the dangers associated with offense helps us resist this temptation. But most people have not been taught the deadliness of offense, so they suffer its affects unwittingly. In order to live the blessed and fruitful life Jesus called us to, we have to remain void of offense—whether that means resisting the temptation of offense or repenting of an offense we've taken.

Years ago, when my wife, Sue, and I were still young in ministry, some friends asked us to dinner to give us a "word from the Lord." At this point in our ministry, we were traveling and had begun distributing free messages, but offerings were not yet covering our expenses—let alone a salary. And quite honestly, we were just as excited about the free meal as we were the word from the Lord.

Dinner went well, and we were enjoying fellowship when this couple finally got around to giving us the "word from the Lord." It went something like this: "The Lord has shown us that three wolves are coming into your ministry who are endeavoring to devour you." Talk about unsettling! Suddenly, the free meal began turning in my stomach.

I had lots of questions about the word. I wanted details like who, when, how, and where. But the couple had no idea. They just gave us the word the Lord had given them and told us to be prepared. Perhaps even more puzzling to me—Sue didn't seem to be concerned. As soon as we got in the car, I asked her what she thought of the word. "Who could possibly want to hurt our ministry?"

My sweet, loving wife looked at me as serious as can be and responded, "I don't know who the third wolf is, but two of them were sitting at the table with us."

I couldn't believe my ears! After recovering our car from the bar ditch, I said, "Honey! How could you say such a thing? They're our friends!" I wasn't trying to condemn Sue, but I could not fathom this couple doing such a thing. After all, they were the ones who had given us the word. Could they really be party to the destruction of our ministry? Sue was unmoved by my outburst. She was actually operating in the discerning of spirits and discerned that the word was coming out of their own hearts.

Two weeks later, that couple and a local pastor in our prayer circle called me a false prophet from the pulpit. They instructed everyone in their congregation to burn my cassette tapes (yes, it was a long time ago!) and never listen to me again. In that moment, I had opportunity to take offense. But had I done so, that offense could have ruined our lives and destroyed the fruitfulness of our ministry.

Sue, too, could have taken offense—at me—for not trusting her discernment in the matter. And that offense would have brought turmoil to our marriage. Instead, we prayed together over it. We judged our own hearts, reminded ourselves of what God had called us to do, and forgave them. We continued to teach the Word as God instructed us and distributed our messages free of charge. As a result, our ministry became more and more fruitful, but over the years, theirs became fruitless.

Dear ones, no person can cause you or your ministry to fail. No one can cause you to become fruitless. Only you can do that by harboring offense. And while this experience was painful, I learned something important—always listen to Sue!

You may have never thought about this, but Christians don't really produce fruit. Christians are the bride of Christ. We are in a husband-wife type of relationship with Jesus, and just like a wife bears children, we—as Christ's bride—bear fruit. Jesus is the one who produces it. Fruit is the by-product of a heart in right relationship with Jesus. It is the proof of our faith working together with His grace.

In Mark 4, Jesus used the Parable of the Sower to teach us how God's Word produces fruit in our hearts and lives. In it, Jesus describes a man who went out to sow seed. As he was sowing, the man's seed fell on different types of ground and produced different results. When Jesus' disciples approached Him about the meaning of this parable, He said that God's Word is like seed and our hearts are like the ground. As God's Word abides in the ground of our hearts, we bear fruit.

So why don't all Christians bear the same amount of fruit in their lives? According to Jesus' parable, the problem lies with the ground. God's Word, the seed, is constant. But of the four types of ground Jesus listed in His parable, only one brought forth fruit *"some thirtyfold, some sixty, and some a hundred"* times what was sown (Mark 4:8, 20 NKJV). Any lack of fruit was not due to the seed, but rather to the condition of the ground. Today, when you see Christians displaying different kinds and amounts of fruit, the variable is always the ground of their hearts.

FOUR TYPES OF GROUND

The first type of ground mentioned in Mark lay "by the wayside." This ground was literally on the side of the farmer's field. It was the path people walked to avoid compacting the farmer's prepared soil and tender, growing plants. Jesus likened this ground to His hearers with hard hearts. *"And these are they by the wayside, where the word is sown; but when they have heard, Satan cometh immediately, and taketh away the word that was sown in their hearts"* (Mark 4:15).

In Matthew's account of this same parable, Jesus said, *"When any one heareth the word of the kingdom, and **understandeth it not**, then cometh the wicked one, and* *catcheth away that which was sown in his heart..."* (Matthew 13:19). When we hear but do not understand God's Word, Satan steals the seed from our hearts. As a result, we bear no fruit.

The second type of ground is stony ground, but I will come back to that shortly. The third ground Jesus mentioned is thorny ground. Seed growing in this area of the field struggled to survive. It had to compete with the weeds for water and light. About these hearers Jesus said,

> *And these are they which are sown among thorns; such as hear the word, and the cares of this world, and the deceitfulness of riches, and the lusts of other things entering in, choke the word, and it becometh unfruitful.*

> —MARK 4:18–19

These things—the cares of this world, the deceitfulness of riches, and the lust of other things—create a toxic environment in our hearts. This environment cancels out the positive affect of God's Word.

The "cares of this world" are distractions like financial burdens, health issues, or employment woes that cause stress and anxiety in our lives. They shift our focus from the things of God and inspire us to worry about the future (see Matthew 6:33–34). The "deceitfulness of riches" refers to the lies we believe about money. First Timothy says it is the love of money that is the root of all evil, not money itself (see 1 Timothy 6:10). Riches are not bad. But trusting them to do God's job of promoting, protecting, and providing for us is. The third "thorn" Jesus mentions in this type of ground is lust. *Lust* is an unhealthy desire for the things of this world. God did not create our hearts for lust. Colossians tells us that lust or covetousness is a form of idolatry, which is worshiping something other than God (see Colossians 3:5). All these things—the cares of this world, deceitfulness of riches, and lust of other things—cancel out the effectiveness of God's Word, and if not dealt with, they will cause us to become unfruitful.

The fourth ground Jesus mentioned is good ground that receives the seed and produces fruit. About these hearers, Jesus said, *"And these are they which are sown on good ground; such as hear the word, and receive it, and bring forth fruit, some thirtyfold, some sixty, and some an hundred"* (Mark 4:20). Hearts that hear God's Word, understand it, and protect themselves from weeds, are exceedingly fruitful! This is the ground we should all strive to become.

Now, back to the stony ground I mentioned earlier. This ground was full of rocks. It had very shallow soil. It might have been a stone border marking the boundary to the farmer's field, or it could have been an area of the field that looked well tilled yet hid a layer of rock just beneath the surface. Of these hearers, Jesus said:

> *And these are they likewise which are sown on stony ground; who, when they have heard the word, immediately receive it with gladness; and have no root in themselves, and so endure but for a time: afterward, when affliction or persecution ariseth for the word's sake, immediately they are offended.*

> —MARK 4:16–17

The trials and persecutions of this life are designed to offend us. Offense is Satan's way of stealing God's Word from our hearts. Yet how many Christians blame God when His Word "isn't working" in their lives?

According to scripture, when we struggle to understand God's Word, when the cares of this world surround us, or when riches deceive us, the seed of God's Word is hindered from working in our hearts. When we become offended because of tribulations, persecutions, and afflictions, we cannot bear fruit. Yet many Christians falsely believe the reason God's Word doesn't work is that God is playing favorites—and they aren't chosen.

Like natural seed, the seed of God's Word is no respecter of persons (see Romans 2:11). It is a respecter of ground. If a seed is sown on concrete, we should not be surprised when it bears no harvest. The seed is not the problem; the ground is. This is actually good news! If our hearts are the problem, they can be fixed. If God was the problem, we'd be toast!

God did not create any of us to be bad ground. He created us to be good ground, ready and eager to bear much fruit. So how do we resist offense and keep Satan from stealing God's Word from our hearts? We must understand the deeper message of Jesus' Parable of the Sower. As children of God, we are called to bear fruit through our relationship with Him (see John 15:8). This is not a burdensome responsibility. It is a joyous process. However, unprocessed offense will keep us from experiencing all God has for us. It will cause us to bear little or no fruit for His kingdom. Fruit comes as a byproduct of peaceful relationship with God and others. Unfortunately, many people do not recognize the enemy's goal with offense. Their lives are full of anger, bitterness, and chaos. As a result, they cannot bear the good fruit God intends.

Look at your own life. Do you know people who have taken offense at God or the church? Do you know any who are offended with their family or friends? Their

spouse? How do these people live? What do their relationships look like? Are they experiencing the joy of their
salvation, or are they bitter and angry? Do they always
seem to be struggling?

What about people in your life who are happy and
bearing fruit in the kingdom (see Galatians 5:22–23)?
How do they live? Do they carry around offense, or are
they kind to others? Do they fill their time bemoaning
how "unfair" life can be, or are they busy being the hands
and feet of Jesus (see Ephesians 2:10)?

Dear ones, we cannot bear the fruit of righteousness
while offended. We must recognize the true source of
offense and the danger it poses in our lives so we can
resist Satan's devices and bear fruit in God's kingdom. It
is for this reason we were called (see John 15:8).

GIVEN FOR OUR INSTRUCTION

In First Corinthians, Paul writes that Old Testament
events—both the good and the bad—were recorded for
our instruction (see 1 Corinthians 10:11). So, let's look at
a few biblical examples of people who took offense and
see how it affected their lives.

Saul, Israel's first king, began his reign in humble obedience to God. But King Saul didn't end that way. Though
he was dearly loved by God, and the Lord's favor was

upon him, Saul allowed offense to negate God's plan for his life. After Saul's continual acts of rebellion and disobedience toward God, God sent the prophet Samuel to correct Saul. On one occasion, Samuel told him,

> *You have done foolishly, you have not kept the commandment of the Lord your God, which He commanded you. For now, the Lord would have established your kingdom over Israel forever. But now your kingdom shall not continue...*
>
> —1 SAMUEL 13:13–14 NKJV

Think about that. God willed nothing but good for King Saul, yet offense robbed him of the blessings and long-term plan God had for his life.

Saul's offense also spilled out on those nearest and dearest to him. David, a loyal servant in Saul's house (and his son Jonathan's best friend), loved and obeyed Saul in everything. He was so successful in serving, loving, and blessing the king that Saul made him commander of his armies. Once, after a successful military campaign, as David's armies were returning to Israel, an impromptu parade broke out. The ladies of Israel came out dancing, singing, and playing their tambourines. Their song is recorded in First Samuel 18. In it, they sang of how Saul had killed thousands but David tens of thousands (see 1 Samuel 18:17). Check out Saul's response.

> *This made Saul very angry. "What's this?" he said. "They credit David with ten thousands and me with only thousands. Next they'll be making him their king!" So from that time on Saul kept a jealous eye on David.*
>
> —1 SAMUEL 18:8–9 NLT

David did nothing to initiate the ladies' celebration, yet Saul was offended. In a moment of anger, he forgot about David's loyal service. He forgot about David's friendship and love toward his son, Jonathan, and his heart filled with jealousy. Saul got so angry that he allowed offense to shift his personality. He became deranged, literally attacking David and trying to kill him multiple times. This needless offense eventually destroyed him and cost Saul everything he had—his kingdom, family, and ultimately, his life (see 1 Samuel 18). That's how serious offense can be.

Interestingly, our next example of offense is David. After rejecting Saul as king, God found David, *"a man after God's own heart"* and anointed David to serve Him in that office (1 Samuel 13:14). It took several years, but finally, in Second Samuel 6, David officially became king.

He conquered the fortress at Zion and made Jerusalem the capital city of Israel. David's heart for God created a longing within him for the Ark of the Covenant, which, in the Old Testament, housed God's manifest presence. So he determined to bring the Ark back to its proper resting place.

In First Samuel 5, just before Saul's reign, the Philistines stole the Ark and placed it in the temple of their false god, Dagon. The stolen Ark brought so much trouble to the Philistines—causing their false god to bow before it (and eventually, breaking off its head and arms), spreading tumors, and causing rat infestations—that they returned it in First Samuel 6 with a trespass offering. Throughout Saul's reign, the Ark lay forgotten in Kiriath Jearim, about ten miles from Jerusalem.

When King David decided to move the Ark back to Jerusalem, he put together a crew of warriors and musicians. David's men put the Ark on a cart and set out for Jerusalem, celebrating as they went. When oxen pulling the cart tripped, a man named Uzzah took hold of the Ark to keep it from falling. Then *"the anger of the Lord was kindled against Uzzah,"* and God struck him dead on the spot (2 Samuel 6:1–7).

David became offended. He could not understand why God wasn't happy that they were bringing the Ark of the Covenant out of obscurity. He became angry with God for not blessing their efforts, and he may have thought God's judgment on Uzzah was unfair. So David parked the Ark at the house of Obed-Edom (see 2 Samuel 6:8–11).

Dear ones, we find no benefit in being offended at God. We cannot judge God's righteousness or holiness in His acts of judgment. We cannot compare His righteousness to our own. He sees and knows much more than we do (see 1 Samuel 16:7). But we can learn much from this incident. God gave the people of Israel specific instructions on how to move the Ark of the Covenant. David and Uzzah did not follow those instructions. I used to think Uzzah simply reached up to keep the Ark from falling, but scripture says he "took hold of it" (2 Samuel 6:6). Uzzah tried to seize the physical manifestation of God's presence. He tried to control God, which cannot be done—even in the new covenant. We do not control the move of God or His glory. We are simply vessels of it, according to His will and instructions.

Yet I constantly hear from people who are confused by circumstances and offended with God, just like David. It is true that God can handle it; He does not get offended when we are offended by Him. But this sort of offense is deadly to us. It will cause us to be unfruitful and lead to bitterness. Hebrews 12:15 says this "root of bitterness" has defiled many of God's people. Thankfully, David was able to process his offense and move forward in relationship with God.

A few months after leaving the Ark at Obed Edom's house, David got news that Obed-Edom was being blessed, along with his entire household. (When the presence of God is manifesting in our homes and churches, it blesses not only us, but everyone around us.) David said, "What am I doing sitting here, pouting?" He'd been whining and asking God, "Why did You do this?" But when David realized his offense had forfeited the blessing of God's presence, he chose to make it right. And this time, he moved the Ark according to God's instructions (see 2 Samuel 6:12–15; 1 Chronicles 15:15).

Instead of trying to control God, David celebrated His presence and offered sacrifices in worship. As the Ark neared Jerusalem, David's wife, Michal (Saul's daughter), saw him dancing before the Lord. Embarrassed at the way her husband was behaving, she took offense at David. But unlike her husband, Michal never processed her offense, and scripture says she *"had no child unto the day of her death"* (2 Samuel 6:13–23). Dear ones, much of the spiritual barrenness we see among believers today can be traced back to unprocessed offense. Satan uses offense to steal God's Word from our hearts and make us fruitless and barren.

Another example of offense from the Old Testament comes from the life of Moses. Moses was a prophet used by God to lead the people of Israel out of Egypt and guide them through the wilderness. Before the children of Israel entered the Promised Land, God wanted to reveal His holiness to them and prepare them for following Him in the middle of a pagan culture.

As the Israelites made their way to the land of promise, they came to a place where there was no water (see Numbers 20:10–12). They'd found themselves in a similar place in the Book of Exodus. There God told Moses to strike a rock to bring forth water for the people (see Exodus 17:1–7). In that instance, Moses had obeyed God, and water had come from the rock—enough to satisfy hundreds of thousands of people and their livestock. Now the Israelites needed water again. This time, however, God told Moses to speak to the rock—not hit it (see Numbers 20:7–8).

The New Testament says that Christ was the rock that followed the people of Israel in the wilderness (see 1 Corinthians 10:4). The first time Moses struck the rock symbolized the crucifixion of Jesus. When Jesus died for our sins, living water came from Him to satisfy every thirsty soul just as natural water came from the rock in the wilderness to satisfy the Israelites' physical thirst. But Christ cannot be crucified a second time.

When God told Moses to speak to the rock the second time the Israelites needed water, Moses disobeyed. He took offense at the Israelites (calling them "rebels") and struck the rock in anger. God, in His mercy, still allowed water to gush forth and minister to the people and animals, but He told Moses that because he did not trust Him (because Moses struck the rock twice), he would not enter the Promised Land (see Numbers 20:12).

Let that sink in. In a moment of anger, this great man of God, who had led the people of God faithfully for years, lost his promised land. He allowed offense to get in the way of his obedience to God, and it cost him dearly! I don't know what your promised land is, but mine is the kingdom of God. And while I may be entering into that promised land gradually, I don't want offense to keep me from experiencing all that God has for me. I want to keep a good heart.

Another interesting example of offense comes from Second Kings 5. Naaman, a famous warrior for the king of Aram, was commander of the joint Aramean and Syrian armies. During a campaign against Israel, he captured a young Israelite girl to serve his wife. Naaman was good to the girl, and when she heard of his leprosy, she told Naaman's wife about a prophet in Israel who could heal him.

As soon as Naaman heard this, he went to his king for permission to travel to Elisha the prophet. In those days, Israel and Aram were at odds with one another, but the king of Aram loved Naaman and gave him permission to go. When Naaman arrived at the place Elisha was staying, a servant greeted him. "I am Naaman," he said. "I'm here to be healed by Elisha. Where is he?"

But Elisha refused to meet with Naaman. Instead, Elisha sent his servant with a message. "Go and wash in the Jordan seven times."

Naaman was offended that Elisha did not personally come out to talk to him or heal him. He stormed off, ready to return home—still a leper. Thankfully, one of Naaman's servants helped him process this offense. Naaman opened his heart to obey the word of the Lord spoken through Elisha, and he went home healed (see 2 Kings 5:1–14). Had Naaman held on to offense, he would have forfeited this blessing.

CHAPTER TWO

HOW OFFENSE OPERATES

*Then He said to the disciples, "It is
impossible that no offenses should come..."*
—LUKE 17:1 NKJV

Jesus taught that offense is inescapable. It will come,
but as believers, filled with His Spirit, we do not have to
be overcome by offense. We can be a people who live at
peace with God and our fellow humans both at home
and within our vocations.

Psalm 119:165 says: *"Great peace have they which love
thy law: and nothing shall offend them."* I used to wonder
where the people of peace who loved God's law were.
It seemed every Christian I encountered was offended
about something or quick to take offense over nothing.
Eventually, I decided that instead of trying to find these
people of peace, I would become one.

Like most people, I used to be offended by everything. But God graciously delivered me from that. He gave me great peace as I learned to love His law and recognize offense early—before it could take root in my heart. God's law is a law of love (see Romans 13:8–10). It works no ill toward its neighbor. It forgives. It values others. It teaches us to "take no offense" as we learn to love others with God's kind of love. Love is the fulfilment of the law.

THREE TYPES OF OFFENSE

Over the years, I have discovered three common types of offense the devil uses to deceive people and steal God's Word from their hearts—imaginary offense, accidental offense, and actual offense. Perhaps the most common is imaginary offense. You may be wondering who in the world would sit around and use their imagination to get offended. But remember what happened with Saul. David loved him and served him loyally. And for a time, Saul loved David in return. But as jealousy rose up in his heart, Saul became suspicious of David. Soon that suspicion morphed into hatred, and Saul became deranged. He lost focus on what he was anointed to do—serve God as a good king—and became fixated on destroying David. Saul's offense destroyed his life and ministry, but it was all in his head.

In Second Corinthians 10, Paul writes about vain "imaginations" or presumptions. He calls these imagined things strongholds that exalt themselves against the truth. And he gives us the cure—to use truth (the Word of God) to pull them down. When we are willing to deal with imaginary offense, when we are willing to take our thoughts captive and bring our minds to the "obedience of Christ," strongholds will crumble (2 Corinthians 10:4–5).

Early in our marriage, most of our issues came from speculative imagination. We'd have a misunderstanding or disagreement over something, and I would just walk off—sometimes for hours. I needed time to process and think through the problem, but I never told Sue that. Every time I left, Sue thought I was leaving for good. I had to mature and learn how to work on the problem with her. And she had to learn to stop assuming the worst. Once we did that, our marriage became immeasurably more fulfilling and peaceful.

The devil doesn't care if offense is imagined. He'll take advantage of any offense—whether it's real or not—to steal God's Word from our hearts and destroy our relationships. If we don't learn to process these things correctly, we, like Saul, will become bitter and barren in life. This happens in ministry all the time. A few people have become offended at me or someone else in the church for no reason at all. Sometimes, the person they're mad at wasn't even involved in what happened!

Once, a lady took offense at something I said during a church meeting. I was preaching about being a new creation in Christ and declaring who we are as a result. At one point, I said, "But we have a dumb head," meaning that we are our own worst enemy. We have a tendency to blame the devil for every bad thing in our lives, but most of our problems come from our carnal, unrenewed minds, not the devil. Well, that's not what this lady heard. She allowed Satan to tempt her into thinking I said she was a "dumb head." Even though I'd already said, "We are the righteousness of God. We are heirs of God and joint heirs with Jesus." When I said, "We have a dumb head," this lady got so mad, she jumped all over her pastor and berated him for inviting me to speak.

But it was an imagined offense. I did not call her a dumb head. I said she had a dumb head. There's a difference. We all have dumb heads sometimes. But it would be rude for me to call you that. You are not a dumb head. You are a child of God. And that's what I said during my message. It took me five to ten minutes to convince that lady I did not call her a dumb head. I called her a new creation. I called her righteous and truly holy. I called her a member of the body of Christ, but Satan nearly stole that Word from her heart. The smartest day you and I will ever have as Christians is the day we realize we are not as smart as we think.

Romans 8:7 tells us that *"the carnal mind is enmity against God: for it is not subject to the law of God, neither indeed can be."* That's why we have to take our thoughts captive. That's why we have to make our minds come to the obedience of Christ (see 2 Corinthians 10:5). We have to die to ourselves and our feelings—just like Jesus did when He chose to go to the cross (see Philippians 2:8).

God's Word calls each of us to be soberly minded— especially leaders (see 1 Peter 5:8; Titus 2; 2 Timothy 4:1– 8). We cannot hold on to negative thoughts about others. So how do we deal with imagined offense quickly, so it doesn't take root in our hearts? We must confront it. One of the best ways to do this is to ask whomever you're struggling with, "Did you say or do this?" or, "What did you mean when you said or did this?" Nine out of ten times, the thing you're struggling with is a misunderstanding. And when you confront the temptation to be offended, you overcome it.

If you're worried about an interaction you've had with someone, go to that person. Ask for clarification, and, if need be, pursue reconciliation. Harboring imagined offense is not worth it. Pursue clarity and move on. The lady who took offense at my "dumb head" comment could have simply asked what I meant when I said we have a dumb head. Instead, she falsely accused me and caused her pastor a lot of grief. Thankfully, she came around once she understood what I was truly saying, and it changed her life. But that imaginary offense could have destroyed her. If she hadn't gotten clarity, she could have falsely accused me for years. She would have sowed seeds that harmed others, and she would have reaped a negative harvest in the years to come.

The second kind of offense is accidental offense. I've been guilty of this, and I'm sure you have, too. We unintentionally hurt family and friends more times than we care to admit. I've forgotten my kid's birthdays—never intentionally. But we get busy. Imagine if I purposely "forgot" my anniversary just to see how Sue dealt with it. That's suicide. Nobody would do that. A young newlywed once asked me, "How do you remember important dates, like your anniversary?" With genuinely good intentions, I said, "Forget it just once, and you'll never forget again."

But if I dug a hole for every accidental offense I caused, I would be digging all day long. I once asked a lady when her baby was due, only to discover she wasn't pregnant. I'll never do that again! I was so embarrassed over that piece of stupid. Can you imagine the offense I created? Of course, I apologized, but I felt terrible. The key to overcoming accidental offenses is to understand that we are all imperfect. We need to walk in love and sow mercy for accidental offenses. Clearly, I have needed a lot of mercy in my life. But I give that mercy as well. If someone accidentally offends me, I do my best to give them the benefit of the doubt.

Some things in life we just need to learn to let go. First Peter 4:8 says, "*...love covers over a multitude of sins*" (NIV). The ability to overlook a transgression is a form of God's love and presence in your life. People make mistakes. They fall short. But if we're easily offended, it's because we don't love. So learn to sow mercy. You may need it someday.

> *Good sense and discretion make a man slow to anger, and it is his honor and glory to overlook a transgression or an offense [without seeking revenge and harboring resentment].*
>
> —PROVERBS 19:11 AMP

The third type of offense is actual offense. In this case, the offended party has read the situation accurately. Someone has truly wronged him or her in a meanspirited way, and it hurt. It may have even harmed that person's reputation. This is the type of offense Jesus refers to in Matthew 18:15 when He says, *"Moreover if your brother sins against you, go and tell him his fault between you and him alone. If he hears you, you have gained your brother"* (NKJV).

This verse should be easy to apply, but it's hard to do in real life. I don't know anyone who actually enjoys confrontation. It's uncomfortable. Most people prefer to avoid it. But it's an important part of a healthy and functioning church. Notice, though, what Jesus said. "If your brother offends you, go to him *alone*." Not to everyone, but to the *one* who offended you. When we don't follow this decree, relationships collapse and more offenses are unnecessarily created.

I once knew a minister who got offended with me for "preaching heresy" and sought to destroy my relationships with other ministers. A good friend told me what this person was saying. So I went to him. (I wished he'd come directly to me instead of going to other pastors, so I knew I had to go to him.) When I lovingly confronted the man, he quickly admitted what he'd done. I asked him what heresy I was preaching, and together we listened to one of my cassette tapes. (Yes, it's been awhile!) As we listened, the man kept saying, "It's coming up in a moment...it's coming up in a moment." But we listened to the whole message, and he couldn't tell me what I'd said in error. The man began to weep. He repented and apologized for what he'd done; unfortunately, some of the pastors took up his imaginary offense and relationships were damaged.

Relationships are important to God. They affect the quality of our lives. (Your life can actually be summed up in the depth of your relationship with God and your relationships with other people.) But relationships can also be hard. We keep those relationships healthy by loving people unconditionally and learning to forgive.

When we are wronged by someone, Jesus said we are to go to that person alone. *"But if he will not hear, take with you one or two more, that 'by the mouth of two or three witnesses every word may be established'"* (Matthew 18:16 NKJV). Jesus did not say to run your brother down before others. He did not say to get two or three people on your side and then crucify your brother with the mob. He said to find two or three independent witnesses who can help you process the offense and reconcile with your brother.

Then Jesus took it a step further. He said:

> *And if he refuses to hear them, tell it to the church.
> But if he refuses even to hear the church, let him
> be to you like a heathen and a tax collector.*

> *Assuredly, I say to you, whatever you bind on earth will be bound in heaven, and whatever you loose on earth will be loosed in heaven.*
>
> —MATTHEW 18:17–18 NKJV

Sometimes the church takes "binding and loosing" out of its original context. We talk about binding the devil here and loosing God's will there. I am not saying this concept cannot be applied in that way, but the binding and loosing Jesus refers to here is dealing with forgiveness and the reconciliation of an estranged relationship.

If someone offends you, go to that person and try to find reconciliation. Don't allow unforgiveness to creep in and destroy your life or anyone else's. Submit to the biblical process. But even if that person is unwilling to reconcile, forgive that person anyway. Then move on.

THE STAGES OF OFFENSE

Dear ones, offense is a choice. But you can also choose to walk with a sober mind. You can choose to sow mercy and forgive. You have the power to lovingly confront a brother or sister over a wrong done. And you have the power to release offense. That is not to say you'll always feel like it. There are times when your feelings will be legitimately hurt. Someone will do or say something that causes emotional trauma, and it will trigger the temptation to take the bait of offense. But if we take the bait, we allow Satan to ensnare us.

In Luke 17:1, Jesus said to the disciples, *"It is impossible that no offenses should come..."* (NKJV). Did you catch that? He said *impossible.* In this life, you will have opportunity to be offended. Yet Jesus also gave us the way out (see 1 Corinthians 10:13).

The Greek word in Luke 17 for offenses is *skandalon.* It means "a trap stick, a snare, or an occasion to fall."[1] In other words, offense is meant to ensnare you. Unresolved offense leads to sin. It causes us to stumble and fall. From the heart, we gossip, slander, and create division and strife. And if we carry that offense long enough, we will become the very thing that offended us.

To me, the most interesting part of *skandalon*'s definition is a "trap stick." A trap stick is the part of a mousetrap that triggers the trap when a mouse touches it. When you set a mousetrap, you put cheese on the trap stick and wait for the unsuspecting victim to enter temptation. When a mouse touches the spring-loaded trap—SNAP! The trap is sprung. The bar slams down and brings sudden death to the unsuspecting victim.

Offense is a trap stick. It ensnares us with anger, hurt, unforgiveness, and bitterness. And it leads to destruction.

So when offense comes, recognize Satan's trap and shout, "I smell cheese! Feet don't fail me now." Then...RUN!

If we don't "smell the cheese"—if we don't recognize when offense is baiting us (or we choose to become offended anyway)—we start walking through three distinct stages of offense. The farther down this path we travel, the harder our heart becomes and the more difficult it becomes to escape the trap.

The first stage of offense is nursing the offense. In this stage, we hold offense close. We cuddle and coddle it. We say, "Poor me. I don't deserve this." Or, "How could they say that about me? How could they do that to me?" In my early years of ministry, when people would get mad over some passing comment I made or something they thought I said in a message, they'd quit the church and I'd go home and pout like a baby. "How could they do that after all I've done for them?" It sounds extreme, but that's what offense looks like. That's what nursing an offense sounds like. It is self-centered.

At this point in the process, offense is trying to take root in our hearts. We're in the trap, but we can still escape. We need only to repent. If we do not repent, our offense will evolve into stage two.

The second stage of offense is where the real danger starts. In this stage, we rehearse the offense. We replay it over and over in our minds, and before long, Satan appears, helping us exaggerate what happened. We assign motivation and guilt to the one who offended us and paint a monstrous picture of their character. As our emotions build, we convince ourselves that our feelings are justified, that we have a right to be angry or hurt. We may even call it "righteous anger." But it is not. It's just a pity party—and the only person who ever comes to a pity party is the devil. I'm talking about imaginary or accidental offense here. Actual offense must be addressed and dealt with differently. Even in actual offenses like child abuse, abandonment, or an unwanted divorce, one must learn to release it to God and renew their mind on God's goodness and restoration.

I know people who are still reliving offenses that happened twenty years ago. For twenty years, the incident has been like late night television replaying clips of the same movie again and again in their minds. When the credits roll, they remember every person involved in the offense and imagine there's a big conspiracy against them. That's what Saul did. He only imagined David doing terrible things to him. None of it was true. He nursed and rehearsed his offense until it consumed him. This self-absorption led to the third and final stage of offense—dispersing offense.

Up to this point, the trap of offense has only affected you. But walking into this third stage will trigger Jesus' warning of Luke 17:1 *"Woe to him through whom* [offenses] *do come"* (NKJV). When we start dispersing offense, when we tell someone "our story" with no regard for the damage it will cause the absent party, we create offense. Instead of seeking help to process the hurt and pursue restoration, we multiply the offense. We cause others to take up offense on our behalf and make them stumble right into Satan's trap (see 1 Corinthians 10:32).

This happens a lot between a husband and a wife. When one has a problem, they run to their family and talk about what a bad thing their spouse did. With only one side of the story, the in-laws side with their child and take up the offense. Even though the couple eventually works it out, the in-laws still carry the offense, and it affects their interactions for years. They will not forgive their child's spouse, and it stresses both of their relationships. This is why Jesus said, *"If your brother sins against you, rebuke him..."* (Luke 17:3 NKJV). He did not instruct us to tell other people about the offense. He does not want us dispersing it. He wants us to work toward reconciliation.

Dispersing offense leads to self-destruction. Again, Matthew 18:15 says, "If your brother sins against you, go and tell him his fault *between you and him alone"* (NKJV).

This confrontation is between you and him alone. Not your friends. Not your family. Not anyone else. Especially not the world through Facebook or Twitter. Offenses dispersed through social media can potentially damage thousands of lives. Imagine the negative harvest off all those bad seeds (see Galatians 6:7–8). Actually, you probably don't have to imagine it. Offense spreads like wildfire, and you can see examples of this devastating harvest throughout our culture. This is not the way God wants us to live. Nursing, rehearsing, and dispersing offense destroys us. But we have another option. We can choose to reverse it.

REVERSING OFFENSE

Jesus did not call us to ignore the offenses we encounter. He never asked us to be super-saints who don't get offended. Instead, He taught us to recognize that offense is a trap, and He showed us the best way to avoid its escalation.

If you encounter something that offends you, take it to God. Instead of nursing those feelings, lay them at the feet of Jesus. God will help you overcome the offense if you do not choose to nurse it, rehearse it, or disperse it.

But what if you've already been ensnared by the trap of offense? Simply repent. Confess it to God and receive

His forgiveness and mercy. And if your heart hurts, give that to God as well. Many times great grief, pain, and brokenness of heart comes with offense. But God is near to the brokenhearted. No matter what has happened to offend you, God can heal you. He will deliver you when you turn to and trust in Him.

> *The Lord is near to those who have a broken heart, and saves such as have a contrite spirit. Many are the afflictions of the righteous, but the Lord delivers him out of them all.*
>
> —PSALM 34:18–19 NKJV

Just as offense has a process, so too breaking free from offense has a process. And it starts with the denying of self. Self is the center of all offense. In Matthew 16:24, Jesus says, *"If any man will come after me, let him deny himself and take up his cross and follow me."* Taking up our cross involves the death of the old self-centered way of life and the taking up of our new life in Christ. Through the power of His cross, we can learn to be God-centered and others-minded. We can follow Jesus rather than the pain and hurt of offense.

In the next several chapters, I'll share more biblical principles for finding freedom from offense and lay out practical steps to help guide you through the process.

CHAPTER THREE

Misunderstanding God's Nature

*The Son radiates God's own glory and
expresses the very character of God...*
—HEBREWS 1:3 NLT

Jesus came to give us a picture of God. He is God's "selfie," if you will. He came to show us God's nature, character, and love. He is not an incomplete picture of God, only showing one side of the Father. Many translations of Hebrews 1:3 call Him the "exact representation" of God (NIV, ESV, Berean, NASB, Christian Standard, HCSB, Weymouth, and others). Colossians declares that He is *"the image of the invisible God, the firstborn over all creation"* (Colossians 1:15 NKJV). Jesus was *"the Word...made flesh"* (John 1:14). He was God's Word with hands, feet, and eyeballs. So we can be confident that if we have seen Jesus—if we have known Him from scripture—we have seen or known the Father (see John 14:7).

Unfortunately, too many Christians have not been taught this simple truth. They do not understand God's nature. They see the curses prescribed in the law and believe God is angry, vengeful, and hard to please. If Jesus did anything, He only placated the Father's wrath. Dear ones, this is just not true. While Jesus did warn us of wrath to come for the disobedient and unbelieving, He never poured out wrath on anyone. He showed us the longsuffering love of God (see Exodus 34:6; Psalm 86:15; 103:8; 145:8; 1 Corinthians 13:4). He showed us God's grace. Jesus is the image of God (see 2 Corinthians 4:4). He never made anyone sick or poor, but constantly extended grace, mercy, and love. He did these things because that is the true nature of God.

Jesus came to show us God's willingness to save, heal, forgive, and restore what sin did to us all. His grace has redeemed us from every curse of the law. Galatians 3:13 says, *"Christ hath redeemed us from the curse of the law, being made a curse for us: for it is written, Cursed is every one that hangeth on a tree."* This is why Jesus came. It's why He died for us. He died to redeem us—to rescue us—from the punishment associated with breaking God's holy law. He not only died for our sins, but He also bore God's wrath for sin. That's grace.

Too many people have been taught that the law revealed God. They think God is responsible for the problems in their lives. That He makes them sick and poor to punish them or teach them a lesson. They do not understand that the cross ended the Old Testament administration of wrath, curses, and punishment for sin. We are now under a new administration of grace and righteousness by faith (see 2 Corinthians 3:7–10).

Romans 3:20 says, *"Therefore by the deeds of the law there shall no flesh be justified in his sight: for by the law is the knowledge of sin."* The law does not reveal God's nature; it reveals sin. That's one of the reasons God gave it. In Romans 7:7, Paul declared: *"...I would not have known sin except through the law. For I would not have known covetousness unless the law had said, 'You shall not covet'"* (NKJV). So we see one of the purposes for the law was to make sin known—to prove to us that we needed saving.

The law revealed sin so we would repent and fall upon God's mercy. It revealed our need for a savior. Jesus is the one who reveals God to us (see John 14:7; Colossians 1:15, 19; Hebrews 1:3). He was God made flesh (see John 1:14). He never made anyone sick or killed anyone's kids. (If you want to learn more about this, my free teaching series on the "Purpose of the Law" and "Righteousness by Faith" go into detail explaining God's love for us and the new covenant we have with Him. I encourage you to download them for free from my website.) Romans 8 reveals God's true nature toward us—a nature of love. It begins:

> *There is therefore now no condemnation to them which are in Christ Jesus, who walk not after the flesh, but after the Spirit. For the law of the Spirit of life in Christ Jesus hath made me free from the law of sin and death. For what the law could not do, in that it was weak through the flesh, God sending his own Son in the likeness of sinful flesh, and for sin, condemned sin in the flesh: that the righteousness of the law might be fulfilled in us, who walk not after the flesh, but after the Spirit.*

—ROMANS 8:1–4

God is not condemning you. Condemnation is punishment. It's negative judgment that "damns" the guilty.[2] God condemned—He punished—sin in the body of Jesus. So now, even in your sin, God is merciful.

Don't misunderstand. God hates sin. Sin is deadly. It has consequences. But God loves you. He will chasten or correct and discipline you over sin, but He doesn't do it in wrath. He disciplines us in love. If you feel condemned, that is not God. It could be your conscience or the devil trying to condemn you, but it's not God. Jesus made us *"free from the law of sin and death"* (Romans 8:2).

God took our sins, put them in the flesh of Jesus, and punished Him in our place. Sin has been dealt with. God is not mad at you. He will never, ever punish or curse you. He poured out His wrath on Jesus. If you don't understand this, you may be tempted to blame God when you go through hardship. But you are God's dearly loved child (see Romans 8:16). He would never do anything bad to you. Look carefully at Romans 8:28. It says, *"And we know that all things work together for good to them that love God, to them who are the called according to his purpose."*

This verse does not say that all things that happen in our lives are good. Nor does it say that all things are from God. It says that God, in His amazing grace and sovereign power, works all things together for our good. He can use the bad that happens to us, but He does not cause it. When we love God and are called according to His purpose, He takes the mess and brokenness of our lives, and like a master kintsugi artist, He makes something stronger and more beautiful out of it.

Dear ones, nothing can separate us from God's love. Not our brokenness. Not our sin. Not hardship or danger or lack (see Romans 8:35). Scripture says, in all these things we are *"more than conquerors through Him who loved us"* (Romans 8:37). When we are born again, we are born of Him—loved and accepted as God's children (see 1 Peter 1:23). Romans 8:14–16 says,

> *For as many as are led by the Spirit of God, these are sons of God. For you did not receive the spirit of bondage to fear, but you received the Spirit of adoption by whom we cry out, "Abba, Father." The Spirit Himself bears witness with our spirit that we are children of God* (NKJV).

And Galatians 4:6 says, *"Because you are sons, God has sent forth the Spirit of His Son into our hearts, crying, 'Abba Father'"* (NKJV).

What a great love God has for us! He rescues us and calls us friends (see John 15:13–14). He gave us a new name, a new identity. We go from children of wrath and enemies of God (see Ephesians 2:3) to members of God's family (see Matthew 12:50). The word *Abba* in Romans 8:15 is a hard word to translate. The closest English word we have for it is *daddy.* God is our heavenly Father, our Daddy God. But do we understand how dearly we are loved? If God loved us when we were sinners by nature and His enemies, how much more does He love us now as His children (see Romans 5:6–10)?

GOD'S GRACE

Unfortunately, when people don't understand this about God's nature, they get offended at His grace. But we cannot earn God's love any more than we could earn our salvation or work our way to holiness. Just like we are made holy by His grace, we are loved, blessed, and healed by grace. This truth offends the legalist. That's why the Pharisees were always mad at Jesus. It offended them to think that all their striving meant nothing in God's sight, and those who didn't "deserve it" could still experience His unconditional love and mercy. Paul talks about this in Romans 9:30–33:

> *What shall we say then? That the Gentiles, which followed not after righteousness, have attained to righteousness, even the righteousness which is of faith. But Israel, which followed after the law of righteousness, hath not attained to the law of righteousness… For they stumbled at that stumbling stone; as it is written, "Behold, I lay in [Zion] a stumblingstone and rock of offence: and whosoever believeth on him shall not be ashamed."*

Jesus—and God's gift of grace—was a rock of offense to law-abiding Jews who'd spent their entire lives trying to live up to God's standard of righteousness, only to fail. This became especially offensive when the Gentiles—who did not have the law—were made righteous through faith. What God meant to be a blessing of grace for all became an offense to His people. And it still happens today. Legalists are constantly offended by the idea that somebody can be made righteous or receive God's blessings without earning them. Yet Titus 3:5–8 says:

> *Not by works of righteousness which we have done, but according to his mercy he saved us, by the washing of regeneration, and renewing of the Holy Ghost; which he shed on us abundantly through Jesus Christ our Saviour; that being justified by his grace, we should be made heirs according to the hope of eternal life. This is a faithful saying, and these things I will that thou affirm constantly, that they which have believed in God might be careful to maintain good works. These things are good and profitable unto men.*

Works are not a bad thing. But we are saved *for* good works, not *by* them. If unconditional love and grace is offensive to you, you are trying to approach God through legalism. And that legalism will cancel out the cross. Paul wrote, "*For Christ sent me not to baptize, but to preach the gospel: not with wisdom of words, lest the **cross of Christ** should be made of **none effect**"* (1 Corinthians 1:17). As powerful as the cross is, we can make it ineffective. That's what happened with the Jews.

In the first decade of its existence, the Church was made up almost entirely of Jews (see Acts 2:41; 4:4). Not until Paul began his missionary journeys did Gentiles begin coming to Christ in large numbers. Yet multitudes of Jews stumbled at the cross and became offended at God's grace. God wanted to save them all, but the Jews canceled out His grace by looking to their own works.

For the preaching of the cross is to them that perish foolishness; but unto us which are saved it is the power of God. For it is written, I will destroy the wisdom of the wise, and will bring to nothing the understanding of the prudent. Where is the wise? where is the scribe? where is the disputer of this world? hath not God made foolish the wisdom of this world? For after that in the wisdom of God the world by wisdom knew not God, it pleased God by the foolishness of preaching to save them that believe. For the Jews require a sign, and the Greeks seek after wisdom:

> *but we preach Christ crucified, unto the Jews a*
> *stumblingblock, and unto the Greeks foolishness;*
> *but unto them which are called, both Jews and*
> *Greeks, Christ the power of God, and the wisdom*
> *of God.*
>
> —1 CORINTHIANS 1:18–24

To the world, the idea of a man dying on a cross for the sins of the world and then being raised from the dead is foolish. People believe they can do good without God (see Matthew 19:17; Isaiah 5:20). They think that if they're holier than their neighbor that's good enough. Some even believe their self-righteousness is superior to God's righteousness. Talk about foolishness!

But to us who are saved, the cross is the power and wisdom of God. Yet, even for those who believe, the cross will become an obstacle when we try to approach God or earn His love on the merits of our own holiness. We see this illustrated in Luke 15:1–2 when the scribes and Pharisees murmured about God's grace. They couldn't believe Jesus would spend time with "sinners."

Throughout the Gospels, tax collectors and sinners eagerly sought out Jesus to hear from Him. But when the Pharisees and scribes saw Jesus eating with sinners, they could not receive from Him. They equated Jesus' association with sinners with a condoning of sin. Jesus didn't condone sin. He came to save sinners. In Luke 15, when the religious leaders murmured about Jesus eating with all the sinners, He took the opportunity to tell a few parables pointing out the immeasurable value of lost things (see Luke 15:3–32). His stories about a lost sheep, lost coin, and lost son illustrate God's care for hurting people.

In the story of the lost sheep, a shepherd left 99 of his sheep to find one that was lost. He then called his neighbors to rejoice with him over the recovery of the one. Some people might accuse the shepherd of neglect, leaving the 99 to search for only one lost sheep. But it actually illustrates his care of each individual sheep. This story gives us a picture of how God cares for and pursues those who go astray. He never gives up but searches until the one lost is found (see Luke 15:7).

In the story of the lost coin, a woman who lost a coin tore her whole house apart to find it. When she did, she called her friends to rejoice with her. God does the same thing when a lost person finds his or her way home. Scripture says all of heaven rejoices over that life (see Luke 15:10).

Jesus also told a story of a son who left home, squandered his inheritance, lost his friends, and wound up starving in a pigpen. I can't imagine anything less appetizing to a Jewish man. (To the Jews, pigs were unclean animals they were forbidden to eat. No Jewish person would have eaten pig meat, much less pig food.) Finally, the son decided to go home. He repented and determined to ask his father for mercy. The young man hoped to become one of his father's hired servants. Jesus said, *"When* [the son] *was yet a great way off, his father saw him, and had compassion, and ran, and fell on his neck, and kissed him"* (Luke 15:20).

The father was not angry with his son. He did not scold or condemn him. I'm sure the father waited for his son every day. He dreamed of his son's return. And as soon as the man saw his lost son walking up the road, he ran to him. He hugged and kissed him, overjoyed at his return. (I'm sure if phones had existed back then, the father would have rushed to his son's side as soon as the son called and asked for help.)

In this parable, the father is a representation of God. The repentant son is a stand-in for you and me. Yet how many religious people paint God as a demanding Father who wants us to beg for mercy at His feet? How many act like the oldest son who, in the parable, was offended at his father's love and bitter at his extravagance toward his younger brother? When the father in Jesus' parable told his servants to bring clean clothes for his son and prepare for a celebration, *"for this my son was dead, and is alive again; he was lost, and is found,"* scripture says the oldest son *"was angry and would not go in"* (Luke 15:22–28). He stood outside and pouted. He complained about not getting fresh clothes and a party. Yet the father showed his great love and extended mercy even to this self-righteous son.

> *Therefore came his father out, and intreated him…Son, thou art ever with me, and all that I have is thine. It was meet that we should make merry, and be glad: for this thy brother was dead, and is alive again; and was lost, and is found.*
>
> —LUKE 15:28, 31–32

The elder son did nothing wrong the whole time his brother was gone—nothing except look to his works to receive favor from his father. The father loved both his sons. But when the younger brother received favor by grace, it became a stumbling block and a rock of offense to the elder—so much so that he could not celebrate the fact that his own brother was alive. That's what offense does. It becomes a burning flame of anger and hurt that devours the good in your heart.

Are you part of God's family, yet offended by grace? Is your life a joyless misery? It may be that you are look-ing to yourself and your works to please God instead of looking to Jesus. If you find yourself in this place, repent. Change your mind and learn to celebrate grace. *"Do not be attracted by strange, new ideas. Your strength comes from God's grace, not from rules about food which don't help those who follow them"* (Hebrews 13:9 NLT).

The Lord understands our weakness. He knows that none of us are above stumbling. Yet He loves us. On the night Jesus was betrayed, He warned the disciples saying, *"All ye shall be offended* [NKJV says, *"made to stumble"*] *because of me this night: for it is written, I will smite the shepherd, and the sheep of the flock shall be scattered abroad"* (Matthew 26:31). Peter didn't believe Jesus. He loved Jesus and didn't think himself capable of being offended. But Jesus knew. He told Peter that before daybreak, he would deny Him three times (see Matthew 26:34). Of course, the Lord was right. Peter did deny Jesus. Peter was distraught when he realized what he'd done, but because of Jesus' love and mercy, he was fully restored (see Matthew 26:75; John 21:15–19).

None of us—even those of us who know Jesus—are immune to offense. We must remain humble and on guard so we do not fall (see Galatians 6:1–5). But if we fall, we have an Advocate with the Father (see 1 John 2:1). Jesus, the Righteous One, has paid the price for our failings, and our heavenly Father waits near the road watching for our return. Like Peter, we must get back up and rejoin the race, knowing that the Word is true. He *"will be merciful to* [our] *unrighteousness, and* [our] *sins and iniquities will [He] remember no more"* (Hebrews 8:12).

CHAPTER FOUR

GETTING OFFENDED AT GOD

And herein do I exercise myself, to have always a conscience void of offence toward God, and toward men.

—ACTS 24:16

I've often wondered how anyone could get offended at God. Not only is He generous and kind, but He is God. What's the point of carrying offense against Him? Yet as a pastor, I've watched hundreds (maybe thousands) of people walk this path. They get offended at God for what they perceive to be His unfulfilled promises. They get offended for not being healed or because their spouses walked out on them. They get offended for not receiving a promotion or an expected answer to prayer. I know people who've served faithfully in ministry, regularly attending church and volunteering, but because they were never hired for a full-time position, they got offended at God and left the church. Why is that? How is that?

Besides misunderstanding God's nature, perhaps the most common reason I've seen for people to get offended at God is that their hearts are unprepared for Christian suffering. I've been a Christian a long time, and I would dare to say that the majority of American Christians do not know how to process the hardships of life. They do not understand persecution or tribulation. They do not understand the world we live in or how Satan uses trouble to rob us of peace and joy. Many of my generation were taught to just grin and bear difficulty. We were taught that suffering is a part of the human condition and that we need to be able to roll with the punches. That view is incorrect. But so is the view that faith in Jesus eliminates all suffering in this life.

As a man, Jesus suffered some things as our substitute, and because of our faith in Him, we don't have to suffer those things. He suffered other things as an example for us to follow. As believers, we need to know which type of suffering is which.

Scripture teaches us how to recognize the kind of suffering we should expect in this life and the kind we should resist. First Peter 4:12 says, "Beloved, think it not strange concerning the fiery trial which is to try you, as though some strange thing happened unto you." But let's be honest. As soon as something difficult happens, we do think it strange. We wonder, *Why is this happening to me? I go to church. I read the Bible. I love God. This should not be happening to me!* But according to First Peter, we're not to find it strange when we go through hardships. The trials of life are common to us all. Our faith doesn't make us immune to those trials. It does not eliminate all tribulation and persecution in this life. Rather, our faith gives us peace and joy in the midst of the difficulties we face.

Look again at this verse in First Peter, this time in the context of verses 13 and 14:

> *Beloved, think it not strange concerning the fiery trial which is to try you, as though some strange thing happened unto you. But rejoice, inasmuch as ye are partakers of Christ's sufferings; that, when his glory shall be revealed, ye may be glad also with exceeding joy. If ye be reproached for the name of Christ, happy are ye; for the spirit of glory and of God resteth upon you: on their part he is evil spoken of, but on your part he is glorified.*
>
> —1 PETER 4:12–14

Do you understand what this is saying? If you are mocked because you love Jesus, rejoice! The Spirit of God must be evident in your life. If it weren't for the Holy Spirit working in you, no one would oppose you. But if Jesus lives in you, the same world that hated Him will hate you. This reality is hard for Christians in our culture to comprehend. Nobody wants to be persecuted. No one wants to be called names. Nobody wants to do the right thing just to experience pushback. But suffering unjustly for doing and saying the right thing is part of the Christian experience. Second Timothy 3:12 promises that all who live godly in this world will suffer persecution. The reason many do not is that they are not living godly lives. Still, we must do what is right—no matter the cost—especially in these last days.

Dear ones, Christian suffering is inevitable in this life. And that's okay. However, Peter also wrote, *"But let none of you suffer as a murderer, or as a thief, or as an evildoer, or as a busybody in other men's matters"* (1 Peter 4:15). And Ephesians 4:28 says, *"Let him who stole steal no longer, but rather let him labor, working with his hands what is good, that he may have something to give him who has need"* (NKJV). I don't think these verses need elaboration. It should be obvious that, as Christians, we don't want to be caught up in the wrong kind of suffering—the kind that comes as a natural consequence of poor choices. Instead, let it be because we follow Christ.

Peter continued, *"Yet if any man suffer as a Christian, let him not be ashamed; but let him glorify God on this behalf"* (1 Peter 4:16). And again, *"For what credit is it if, when you are beaten for your faults, you take it patiently? But when you do **good and suffer,** if you take it patiently, this is commendable before God"* (1 Peter 2:20 NKJV).

Have your kids ever whined about reaping the consequences of their disobedience? As a parent, how do you respond in that moment? If you're anything like me, you probably think, *You should have considered that before you disobeyed.* But how many of us do the same thing in our relationship with God? How many whine and complain when reaping the consequence of our disobedience to God? Even if we "take it patiently," as scripture says, do we recognize that our suffering is a direct result of our bad decision—a harvest off our seed sown—and not a judgment from God? On the other hand, if we suffer from doing good, do we endure it with patience as scripture says? Or do we respond with indignation? Doing what is right does not mean everything will work out perfectly. But God sees the wrong done to us. He also sees our response to that wrong. Are we responding correctly?

Patient endurance of suffering is a foreign concept in our culture—and even in some of our churches. It's not that God desires for people to mistreat us. He's not okay with people being mean or causing us harm. However, He has called us to love others even when they aren't loving toward us. Matthew 7:12 says, *"Do to others what you would have them do to you"* (NIV). It does not say, "Do to them as they have done to you." Suffering happens when you love the unlovely. It's an unescapable fact of this fallen world. But this denying of self is what makes us disciples of Christ. *"For to this you were called, because Christ also suffered for us, leaving us an example, that you should follow His steps"* (1 Peter 2:21 NKJV).

We are called to do what is right and to say what is right, no matter the cost. That's what Christ did, and He is our example.

TYPES OF CHRISTIAN SUFFERING

Let's look at three types of Christian suffering and learn how to respond properly to each by faith.

1. SUFFERING AS OUR SUBSTITUTE

Jesus came to Earth to live and die as our substitute. He suffered the penalty for our sin so we wouldn't have to. Sin is still dangerous. It still has consequences, but when we are in Christ, we do not need to fear suffering from God. God will not turn on us or harm us in any way. His new covenant promises: *"I will be merciful to their unrighteousness, and their sins and their iniquities will I remember no more"* (Hebrews 8:12; see Jeremiah 31:34). God promises that when we sin, He will not respond in wrath. His attitude toward us is mercy—not separation, punishment, or condemnation. Unrepented sin does create suffering, but not from God. Thanks to Jesus' substitutionary sacrifice, sin can no longer separate us from God.

Jesus also bore our sicknesses on the cross (see Matthew 8:17). Isaiah 53:5 and First Peter 2:24 tell us that *"by His stripes we are healed"* (NKJV). That doesn't mean we won't face sickness or disease in this world. It means the price for our healing is paid. We may have to fight sickness in this life, but we don't have to yield to it. Jesus suffered sickness, pain, and disease so that you and I can be healed.

Second Corinthians 8:9 tells us that Jesus also became poor that we *"through His poverty might become rich"* (NKJV). Jesus suffered poverty as our substitute. Now, by faith, we can experience God's kind of prosperity. God's kind of prosperity is all-encompassing. It goes beyond finances to include our health, the relationships in our marriages and families, our emotional well-being, our vocations. God is interested in everything that touches our lives, and He wants us to experience prosperity in each aspect of it (see 3 John 2).

Jesus suffered all these things for us as a substitute. He was separated from God at the cross (see Matthew 27:46). He took the punishment for our sin (see Isaiah 53:5). He bore our sickness and poverty (see Matthew 8:17; 2 Corinthians 8:9). And He was condemned so we could be free (see Romans 8:1–4). Now, through faith in Him, we do not have to suffer these things. Instead, when we submit ourselves to God and resist the devil, he must flee (see James 4:7). Hallelujah!

2. SUFFERING AS AN EXAMPLE

Jesus also suffered some things for us as an example to follow. The world rejected Jesus for doing the right thing. They ridiculed Him for representing His Father well. We should expect no less (see Matthew 24:9). When we suffer for doing right or being a good witness, we should rejoice, knowing we are suffering as Christ did.

In Philippians 3:10, Paul wrote that he wanted to *"know* [Christ], *and the power of his resurrection, and the fellowship of his sufferings."* Jesus fellowships with us and we with Him in Christian suffering. And according to Paul's writings in Romans, we can expect that if we suffer with Him, we will also be glorified with Him (see Romans 8:17). As a believer, when I am falsely accused or laughed at and called names because I believe God's Word and follow Jesus, I must suffer those things patiently and cheerfully, knowing that God is pleased with me, and trusting Him to reward me.

3. SUFFERING AS A CONSEQUENCE

Some suffering in this life comes as a consequence of others' decisions. In case you weren't aware, in this life the consequences of sin affect both the guilty *and* the innocent. God gave us all a free will. If people choose to do something wrong, the seed of their actions will eventually reap a bad harvest. A lot of suffering in this world comes as a result of bad decisions—whether ours or someone else's. I know that feels unfair. We all struggle to understand why God allows things to happen that are not His will. But we can rest in the promise of Galatians 6:7–8, which says:

> *Be not deceived; God is not mocked: for whatsoever a man soweth, that shall he also reap. For he that soweth to his flesh shall of the flesh reap corruption; but he that soweth to the Spirit shall of the Spirit reap life everlasting.*

Though it is God's will to bless us—even in the darkness caused by fallen humans—the good that God provides, in His grace, will be corrupted if we sow to the flesh. When we sin and cause others to suffer, our response should be repentance—both before God and whomever we sinned against. But we also must receive our forgiveness knowing that He is faithful and just. We are forgiven, and despite the sin we may have committed, we can walk with confidence before God (see 1 John 1:9; Hebrews 4:16).

When others sin and cause us to suffer, we must forgive them—whether or not they request it. We must trust God's righteous judgment and His nature as the Righteous Judge (see 2 Timothy 4:8). One day, Jesus will balance the scales. God's plan will be accomplished. At the Lord's appearing, the sin that brought suffering to the masses will be addressed, and He will reward those who have suffered unjustly in this dark world. A new heaven and earth will come. Righteousness will reign. So let us not become offended at God. He is not guilty. He does not create or cause suffering. He is our answer, not our problem.

FALSE PERCEPTION OF FAVORITISM

Just as people misunderstand God's nature and Christian suffering, some get offended at God because they believe

He engages in favoritism. From a human perspective, life often seems unfair. Sometimes it is. But sometimes that feeling is just a result of our narrow perspective.

Jesus told a parable in Matthew 20 about a man who hired workers for his business. This man hired some of his workers at six o'clock in the morning and promised them a day's wage. As the day progressed, he realized he needed more help, so the man hired more workers at nine o'clock, noon, three o'clock in the afternoon, and five o'clock—all for a day's wage. The workers he hired last only worked for an hour, but the owner still paid them the agreed upon amount. Those who were hired first got upset. They complained that the owner's treatment was unfair. They'd worked all day in the heat and deserved more pay than those who worked only a short time.

The owner responded, "Didn't you agree to work for this amount? I have not wronged you. If I want to pay the other workers the same amount, that's my right and my business" (Matthew 20:1–16, my paraphrase).

The owner in Jesus' story was not being unfair or showing favoritism. He was simply a generous man of his word. Sometimes the mercy of God looks like that. If you've been working hard to serve God, it might feel unfair when someone "new" to the faith begins receiving recognition and blessing. You might question God when those in your circle appear more blessed than you. You might think, *What did I not do to get that blessing? Why are they getting that? I deserve to be blessed if that person is being blessed.* But that's the wrong attitude. The Bible says that God *"makes His sun rise on the evil and on the good,"* and sends rain *"on the just and on the unjust"* (Matthew 5:45 NKJV). It can sometimes look like God is showing favoritism, but the bottom line is, He's just good to everybody.

God is not mean-spirited. Regardless of who you are or what you've done, God has made a way for everyone to be saved—and He saves all with the same benefits. There are not many ways to God. There are many ways into hell. Jesus said,

> *Enter by the narrow gate; for wide is the gate and broad is the way that leads to destruction, and there are many who go in by it. Because narrow is the gate and difficult is the way which leads to life, and there are few who find it.*
>
> —MATTHEW 7:13–14 NKJV

Jesus is the only way to heaven (see Acts 4:12). Reliance on His work is your only hope of salvation. God is not impressed by your works. His blessings are not based on how long you've been doing the right thing. They are based on His grace worked by Christ's obedience on the cross. Whether you turn to God when you are five years old or surrender to Him on your deathbed, Jesus saves wholly and completely.

All has been done that needs to be done. Jesus, who is *"the way, the truth, and the life,"* has made each of us right by faith (John 14:6; Ephesians 2:8). He has cleansed us with His blood. Now we all get the same wages, regardless of when we come into His kingdom, because He is a good and generous God—a God who keeps His Word.

VOID OF OFFENSE TOWARD GOD

So how do we stay void of offense toward God? First, we must recognize that the temptation to take up an offense—even against God—is a universal experience. We should not feel condemned over it. John the Baptist, one of the greatest prophets of the entire Bible, was once tempted to become offended at God (see Matthew 11:2–11).

At the end of John's ministry, he was imprisoned for speaking the truth to Herod. While there, his confidence began to waver. He wanted to make sure that his ministry had not been in vain, that Jesus was the Messiah. John didn't want to die wondering if he had fulfilled his destiny. So he sent his disciples to Jesus to ask if He was the one they had been waiting for or if someone else was coming.

Jesus told John's disciples to take a report back to John of all they saw while with Jesus: *"The blind receive their sight, and the lame walk, the lepers are cleansed, and the deaf hear, the dead are raised up, and the poor have the gospel preached to them"* (Matthew 11:5). These words were a reflection of Isaiah's prophecy about the Messiah. They were meant to cheer John and strengthen his faith. Jesus added, *"And blessed is he, whosoever shall not be offended in me"* (Matthew 11:6). One translation says, *"Blessed is he who is not offended because of Me"* (NKJV). Dear ones, if John the Baptist had to be told this, we may also need to hear it.

We should also recognize that our offense—whether directed toward God or people—is a choice. In Acts 24, Paul defended himself before Governor Felix regarding his unjust imprisonment. Paul said he had hope in God for, *"there shall be a resurrection of the dead, both of the just and unjust. And herein do I exercise myself, to have always a conscience void of offence toward God, and toward men"* (Acts 24:15–16).

This is profound. As a whole, we don't see God's negative judgment in the earth today because Jesus bore that judgment on the cross. (There are limited exceptions. For example, God judged Ananias and Sapphira as a warning and course correction for the church in Acts 5:1–11. He also judged Herod, in Acts 12:23, who was eaten by worms as a warning to the world and a call to recognize the true King. This judgment also foretold the judgment that awaits those who refuse to acknowledge Jesus as Lord.) But a day is coming when Jesus will return to judge the whole world in righteousness. Paul explained that he had to exercise himself in this hope. He had to remind himself that Jesus was coming back, and everything would work out in the end. No one would get away with anything.

The word *exercise* in Acts 24 means, "to train or strive."[3] What Paul faced wasn't easy. Neither was his decision to hope. He gave his life serving Jesus, yet was afflicted beyond what most of us can imagine. He was stoned, shipwrecked, beaten, and abandoned. He was wronged by his government and imprisoned unjustly, then had to defend himself before the governor. I am sure Paul was tempted to be offended at God. Perhaps he thought, *Is this what I get for preaching the gospel?* But through it all, he disciplined himself to keep free from offense. He reminded himself that, in the end, all would be judged righteously. Those who sought his harm would be held to account. No one would get away with anything. This truth helped Paul avoid offense and maintain a godly attitude in the midst of suffering. It gave him a right perspective toward both God and man. And if Paul could do it, so can we!

CHAPTER FIVE

FACING A CULTURE OF OFFENSE

...many will be offended, will betray one another, and will hate one another. Then many false prophets will rise up and deceive many. And because lawlessness will abound, the love of many will grow cold.
—MATTHEW 24:10–12 NKJV

If you've been a Christian for any length of time, you've probably heard someone mention the End Times. Or perhaps "argue about the End Times" would be more accurate. It seems everyone has a different opinion about this era in history. But Jesus said something in Matthew 24:4 that most people skim over: *"Take heed that no man deceive you."*

Jesus warned that deception would be a big part of living in the End Times, yet no one seems to be watching for it. In today's political climate, government leaders, news pundits, and others gain power by deceiving the masses through manufactured offense. They politicize science and issues of race, gender, and sexual orientation to create narratives of offense. But they're not actually concerned about such things. They're only trying to create division and strife amongst the people so they can usurp power.

Though there is godly division between faith in Jesus and unbelief, right and wrong, good and evil, Christ and the spirit of anti-Christ; God did not send Jesus to separate people on the basis of race, social-economic status, political affiliation, or gender (see Matthew 10:34–39). Yet, Jesus said in the last days, *"Many shall come in my name, saying, I am Christ; and shall deceive many"* (Matthew 24:5). In other words, the deception of offense would work. False saviors—whether individuals or government entities—would be presented to "rescue" culture from threat of war, famine, and disease. And people would be gullible enough to believe them. But Jesus said:

> *See that ye be not troubled: for all these things*
> *must come to pass, but the end is not yet. For*
> *nation shall rise against nation, and kingdom*
> *against kingdom: and there shall be famines,*

and pestilences, and earthquakes, in divers places.
—MATTHEW 24:6–7

As followers of Christ, we cannot freak out every time there is an earthquake or we hear of a new virus or coming plague. The world freaks out like these things should not be happening. But Jesus told us earthquakes would occur. He said there would be famine and pestilence, plagues and disease. These are all signs of the End Times. Whether you've realized it or not, COVID-19 falls under these warnings. Our world's system has used COVID-19 to instill fear and usurp freedom. But Jesus told us not to let these things trouble us. We need to respond to these occurrences in faith, not fear or worry. We need to recognize the unreasonable responses to this virus (which have ranged from shutting down our economy to closing schools and placing citizens on house arrest) for what they are—tactics to collect power for the elite and convince people that government can be their "savior."

Yet Jesus said these things are just the *"beginning of sorrows"* (Matthew 24:8). He continued: *"Then shall they deliver you up to be afflicted, and shall kill you: and ye shall be hated of all nations for my name's sake"* (Matthew 24:9).

Nobody wants to read that. And honestly, it's still hard for me to wrap my mind around, but one day, nations will hate those who love Jesus. They'll hate those who honor the Bible. They'll hate those who do good and love truth. And many Christians will be killed for His name's sake. We may be experiencing censorship and de-platforming right now, but that is only the beginning of sorrows. Just think. If people offended by the truth can make us socially disappear today, why would we think that one day they won't also try to make us physically disappear? And it all goes back to offense. People are offended by God's Word. They are offended by His promise of healing and protection. They don't want to rely on something they cannot see or prove. They don't want to acknowledge God or His Word, for then they would have to submit to it.

But God's people are called to a kingdom mindset. While we are in the world, we cannot be of it (see John 17:6–19). We cannot allow the politics of anger and hatred to offend us. Jesus said, in these last days, *"Shall many be offended, and shall betray one another, and shall hate one another"* (Matthew 24:10). And then He repeated the warning that many false prophets would arise to deceive the multitudes (see Matthew 24:11). Often, when we think of false prophets, we expect them to rise out of the church. But a false prophet is anyone who claims that he or she can save the world. It's the spirit of anti-Christ—a false Christ, a false solution.

Jesus went on to say, *"And because iniquity shall abound, the love of many shall wax cold. But he that shall endure unto the end, the same shall be saved"* (Matthew 24:12–13). Notice the two signs Jesus gave believers of the End Times. He said many would be offended, and love would "wax cold." The Greek word translated as love in this verse is *agapē*.[4] This is God's kind of love. And according to First Corinthians 13:4–5, *agape* suffers long and is kind. It doesn't envy or boast. It is not proud or rude. Agape love is not selfish, self-promoting, or easily angered. It is not the kind of "love" the world promotes. But it is the kind of love Jesus said Christians would allow to "wax cold" in their hearts.

Instead of nurturing love and enduring to the end, in the last days, Christians, like the world, will take offense at everything. May that not be said of us! Let us instead be inspired by the words of Philippians to let *"your love...abound yet more and more in knowledge and in all judgment; that ye may approve things that are excellent; that ye may be sincere and without offence till the day of Christ"* (Philippians 1:9–10). Paul encouraged the church at Philippi to not let their love wax cold. He charged them to love others and guard their hearts from offense.

Just as then, the only way for us to stay free of offense today is to abound in God's kind of love. First John 4:8

says that *"God is love,"* so knowing Him is the only way to know true love. This means that our ability to love grows as our relationship with God grows. God's kind of love is a foreign concept to this world. It's a foreign concept to our flesh. Love is not an emotion or a feeling. (Though it can affect our emotions—even to the point of healing the hurt created by offense.) Love is a choice. We show love when we choose to do the right thing. We abound in love when we choose God's way over our feelings. Paul encouraged us all to be sincere in this: To not let our emotions rule our decisions, but to choose to keep our hearts free from offense and aligned with the truth until the day of Christ. Then we will be *"filled with the fruits of righteousness, which are by Jesus Christ, unto the glory and praise of God"* (Philippians 1:11). Though the world gives into offense, when our love abounds in knowledge and judgment, we are free from offense and filled with the fruit of righteousness!

OFFENDED BY THE TRUTH

Early in ministry, I mistakenly thought everyone wanted truth. How naïve I was! Many people—national media included—do not care about truth. They only care about what will advance their agenda or position. In some cases, they are actually afraid of the truth and do everything they can to hide it. They are people *"who by their unrighteousness suppress the truth"* (Romans 1:18 ESV). It was a rude awakening for me when I realized how biased the national news media had become, and worse, when I discovered that multitudes of people in the church regularly rejected truth. Peter wrote about this in his second letter.

> *Wherefore also it is contained in the scripture, Behold, I lay in [Zion] a chief corner stone, elect, precious: and he that believeth on him shall not be confounded. Unto you therefore which believe he is precious: but unto them which be disobedient, the stone which the builders disallowed, the same is made the head of the corner, and a stone of stumbling, and a rock of offence, even to them which stumble at the word, being disobedient: whereunto also they were appointed.*
>
> —1 PETER 2:6–8

God's Word is a precious stone to those who believe. But to the disobedient, it is a rock of offense that causes people to stumble. The Word puts obstacles in the path of unbelief. Consider tithing as an example. I've never had a tither get offended when I preach about tithing (or "first fruits" as it is spoken of throughout scripture). Those who are enlightened know that we don't belong to ourselves (see 1 Corinthians 6:19–20). Everything we have, everything we are, belongs to God. So when the Word says, *"Bring ye all the tithes into the storehouse,"* and, *"Honor the Lord with thy substance, and with the first fruits of all thine increase"* (Malachi 3:10; Proverbs 3:9), those who love Jesus count that Word as precious and choose to obey it—even when they don't fully understand it. It's the people who don't want to tithe that stumble at this Word. They become offended, looking for any excuse—whether people's misrepresentation of scripture or a preacher's abuse of prosperity—to justify their disobedience.

I will be the first to admit that there have been abuses in sharing on the subject of prosperity. Many teachers still misrepresent tithing, incorrectly attaching God's wrath to a failure to tithe. We are no longer under the Old Testament law of tithing that curses those who do not tithe. But the principle of tithing, which came before the law and is still applicable after the law, is in effect (see Genesis 14:18–20). This principle attaches a blessing to tithing. Does that make the word we preach a "prosperity gospel?" No. There is only one gospel—the gospel of the Lord Jesus Christ. But part of that gospel message is that God wants us to prosper. If that offends you, it's because you are disobedient to the Word and have stumbled at the truth. Here's another example. Only those who quit church get offended when you quote Hebrews 10:25: *"Not forsaking the assembling of ourselves together, as the manner of some is; but exhorting one another: and so much the more, as ye see the day approaching."*

I could go on and on about offense in the church. But disobedience and offense are not limited to the church. Try sharing God's Word in our culture. You will be attacked by the national media. You will be censored by Silicon Valley tech gods and excommunicated from social media platforms. With few exceptions, anyone in power who speaks truth—even twenty-five percent of the time—is destroyed by our culture. Our culture hates truth. People don't want to know what God's Word says, because then they'd have no excuse for disobeying it.

You see, truth is not relative. It's not something you or I can personally determine. There is no "your truth" or "my truth." Morality is not subject to popular belief or "cultural evolutions." It cannot be determined by majority vote. Truth is absolute. It is eternally established by God. It can only be discovered and submitted to by us. When Jesus stood before Pontus Pilate, Pilate asked if He was a king. Jesus explained that though He was king, He came to the world for one purpose—to bear witness to the truth. And *"...everyone who is of the truth hears My voice"* (John 18:37). Pilate didn't like that answer. *"What is truth?"* he asked (John 18:38). How sad. A high-ranking political official was staring Truth in the face and couldn't recognize it. Yet how many recognize truth today? Most are offended just being in the proximity of truth.

Consider the eternal truth of sexual purity. People who love truth don't get offended when I talk about God's definition of marriage. They don't get offended when I say there are only two genders. They don't get offended when I talk about sexual purity. Only the disobedient do that. But scripture is clear. God created marriage, and only He can define it. Since the creation of the world, marriage has been between a man and a woman. Even Jesus said,

> *But from the beginning of the creation God made them male and female. For this cause shall a man leave his father and mother, and cleave to his wife; and they twain shall be one flesh.*

> —MARK 10:6–8

Male and female were designed by God, with marriage—male and female becoming one flesh—a part of that divine design (see Genesis 1:27; 2:24). Yet if I say a certain sexual activity, like homosexuality, is perverse, people will come out of the woodwork to voice their offense! They do this because the Word of God has become a stumbling block to them.

The older I get, the more aware I become of people who love lies. (Some even make a living off lying!) Truth offends them because it exposes their lies. To these people, the truth is so terrible they'll sue whoever brings truth to light. And they'll do whatever they can to destroy that person's reputation—even taking them all the way to the Supreme Court.

Psalm 119:165 says, *"Great peace have they which love thy law: and nothing shall offend them."* Love for and obedience to God's Word frees us from offense. But if we don't get established in the Word of God, the devil will deceive us. He will cause us to believe a lie and blame God for the problems we face in life. That deception will rob us of the hope of God's promise to balance all accounts and create a new heaven and new earth in which righteousness dwells (see 2 Peter 3:13). It will rob us of the promise from Romans 8:17 that says if we suffer with Jesus, we will also be glorified with Him.

Dear ones, the glory that is coming far outweighs the suffering we experience in this world! God will be true to His Word (see Jeremiah 1:12). He will reward us for all we endure in this life for His name's sake. As Christians in this hour, we are called to persevere, to stand strong in faith and endure to the end (see Matthew 24:13). That's how we keep from being offended by the truth.

Jesus said, *"Blessed are they which are persecuted for righteousness' sake: for theirs is the kingdom of heaven"* (Matthew 5:10). The only persecution most of us will face will be by those in our own circle. Some of us may be persecuted by the media or "rival" political parties. But in other parts of the world, Christians are persecuted unto death. Many are threatened and imprisoned. They cannot worship freely. Some cannot even share their faith without fear of execution. We can thank God that at least in America we are not executed for standing on God's Word. And praise God, we are seeing the tide turn in America! Because of prayer and a newfound love for truth, people are beginning to see the consequences of all the lies, deception, and offense our political leaders have propagated.

I believe we are in the early signs of a third great awakening. God's people are being awakened to the truth, awakened so they do not fall for Satan's trap of offense. Of course, there will be people who get offended when we stand up for godliness and who choose to persecute us. Scripture testifies to that saying, *"All that will live godly in Christ Jesus shall suffer persecution. But evil men and seducers shall wax worse and worse, deceiving, and being deceived"* (2 Timothy 3:12–13). It continues by telling us what our response to that persecution should be. *"But continue thou in the things which thou hast learned and hast been assured of, knowing of whom thou hast learned them"* (2 Timothy 3:14).

As Paul assured a young pastor, Timothy, we must stay the course. We must continue to be obedient to God's Word, regardless of the pushback or persecution we receive. No one likes offending others. (I take that back. There are people in our culture who seem to enjoy it.) *I* do not like offending others. And I assume you don't either. But if God's Word offends, that is on the offended, not on us. Jesus never got offended when the world reviled Him, and He is our ultimate example.

> *"Who committed no sin, nor was deceit found in His mouth"; who, when He was reviled, did not revile in return; when He suffered, He did not threaten, but committed Himself to Him who judges righteously; who Himself bore our sins in His own body on the tree, that we, having died to sins, might live for righteousness—by whose stripes you were healed.*
>
> —1 PETER 2:22–24 NKJV

When the world is offended because we stand up for the truth, we do well to rise above offense as Jesus did.

Jesus never caused offense on purpose or for political gain. He never used offense to promote His agenda. However, His love for truth (and the fact that He is Truth Incarnate) created a lot of offense. There was no indifference around Jesus. Everywhere He went, He either caused a revival or a riot. No one could remain neutral. Those in His circle either ran toward truth or away from it. But Jesus never took offense at their offense. Think about that.

In the Gospel of John, we see Jesus making some hard statements about Himself that offended the Jews. Jesus declared that He was "manna" and "bread from heaven." He even said that unless *"you eat My flesh and drink My blood, you have no life in you"* (John 6:41–59). Let's look at His disciples' response.

> *Therefore many of His disciples, when they heard this, said, "This is a hard saying; who can understand it?"...* [And Jesus] *said to them, "Does this offend you? What then if you should see the Son of Man ascend where He was before?"*
>
> —JOHN 6:60–62

In other words, "Why are you offended? This isn't even the hardest thing I've said!"

Jesus had to deal with His own disciples getting offended at truth. Yet, He didn't take it personally. He didn't get offended at them. He didn't withhold more of the truth. I'm not sure I could say I've always been that Christ-like when people took offense at my preaching, especially around the message of grace and truth. I know there've been instances when I've taken it personally or allowed my feelings to get hurt. (Praise God, I'm learning not to do that!)

Years ago, I was ministering in a service when a man got up—in the middle of my message—and cussed me out as he left the sanctuary. He called me all kinds of names (not all of which were true...let it go!). But I was able to overcome it quickly because it was so obviously demonic. In another situation, a pastor who invited me to speak at his church for a three-night meeting verbally assaulted me every night during his introduction. He had such an offense against TV preachers (and I was on a couple of stations at the time) that I think he specifically invited me as a way to express his offense to his congregation. Each night during the offering, this pastor would claim that TV preachers were just after money. He assumed I was one of those preachers. What happened at that church was so bizarre, I'm glad I had witnesses there to testify of what took place. Anyway, I refused to take offense. I'm not saying I wasn't tempted! But I preached my heart out to those people, blessing them the best way

I knew how. And after the meeting, I sowed the entire offering back into the church just to show them that not all TV preachers were after people's money. I don't share this story to boast in me, but to show how we can combat offense like Jesus did.

> *But I say unto you which hear, Love your enemies, do good to them which hate you, Bless them that curse you, and pray for them which despitefully use you.*
>
> —LUKE 6:27–28

CHAPTER SIX

A GOOD DEFENSE AGAINST OFFENSE

*For the weapons of our warfare are not
carnal but mighty in God for pulling down
strongholds, casting down arguments and
every high thing that exalts itself against the
knowledge of God, bringing every thought
into captivity to the obedience of Christ.*

—2 CORINTHIANS 10:4–5 NKJV

God has given us spiritual weapons (and practical tools) to combat the stronghold of offense in our lives and culture, and it starts with a good defense. The scriptures teach us how to both avoid and overcome offense. Jesus even used the entire seventeenth chapter of Luke to address this issue. Let's take a look.

In Luke 17:1, Jesus told His disciples, *"It is impossible that no offenses should come, but woe to him through whom they do come!"* (NKJV). Many people try to create a perfect, stress-free life. But in a world affected by sin and Satan, we cannot escape imperfection. In this life, it is impossible to be married without being tempted by offense. Misunderstandings happen every day. It is impossible to have kids without facing offense. Kids don't always obey, and at some point, they will likely embarrass you. The same can be said of siblings, parents, and other relatives. You and I will have opportunity in this life to take offense at the things people say or do—whether we're on the job, in the church, or at home. We will never find the perfect job or perfect boss. We will not have perfect children or a perfect spouse. We can't even expect that perfection of ourselves. Anyone who says different is simply not being honest. Jesus said it is impossible to live on this planet and not face offense.

But He also said, *"...Woe unto him, through whom they come!"* The Greek word translated here as *woe* is an exclamation of grief.[5] Grief and sorrow follow the person who brings offense. It would be better for that person, Jesus said, *"that a millstone were hanged about his neck, and be cast into the sea"* (Luke 17:2). Can you imagine that? Offense is so deadly that its consequences are worse than drowning in a pair of concrete shoes!

In the mind of God, it is one thing for a person to fall into sexual perversion or any other sin—even the sin of offense. It's another to teach little children to celebrate that sin. To defile the moral innocence of a child or young believer is terrible. And according to this verse, it warrants multiplied consequences of grief and sorrow. Unfortunately, many offended people don't know this verse. They are not content to destroy their own lives. They want to take others down with them. As believers, we must avoid this destructive behavior. Thankfully, God has given us the tools to do it.

THE POWER OF FORGIVENESS

It begins by taking *"heed to yourselves"* as Jesus said in Luke 17:3. If we would spend more time taking heed to ourselves instead of paying attention to what everybody else is doing, where they're going, or what new thing they are getting, we'd be amazed at how good our lives truly are.

> *Take heed to yourselves: If thy brother trespass against thee, rebuke him; and if he repent, forgive him. And if he trespass against thee seven times in a day, and seven times in a day turn again to thee, saying, I repent; thou shalt forgive him.*
> —LUKE 17:3–4

Our first defense against offense is forgiveness. We are not meant to carry worry and unforgiveness through life. When others offend us, we are commanded to forgive—no matter how many times they have hurt us. But notice Jesus' disciples' reaction to this command. (It's probably similar to your own.) *"Increase our faith!"* (Luke 17:5). This response fascinates me. Prior to this moment, Jesus had commanded the disciples to heal the sick, cleanse the leper, raise the dead, and cast out demons (see Matthew 10:8). Not once did they respond, "Lord, increase our faith!" You'd think those instructions would have created an awareness of their need for more faith. But no. Only when Jesus said "forgive each other" did panic set in.

Whether or not forgiving those who have wronged you feels out of reach, faith is the answer. But like the disciples, we don't need more faith. We need to act on the faith we already have (see Luke 17:6). I don't know about you, but that is motivating to me. I want to have peace in life. I don't want to become a vehicle for offense. I want to be a vessel of honor. I want to show others God's love, kindness, and goodness. And I believe you do, too. Otherwise, you wouldn't be reading this book. The only way that's possible is to walk in forgiveness by faith—a faith I already have.

If you're struggling with forgiveness, if bad stuff has happened to you, if your family has hurt you, if the church has hurt you—forgiveness can seem impossible. It may feel like you need more faith. But according to Jesus words, you have enough faith to operate in forgiveness. You don't need more; you just need to learn how to act on the faith you have.

Forgiveness is our greatest defense against offense. In Matthew 18, Peter asked, "Lord, how often shall I forgive my brother? Up to seven times?" Jesus said, "Peter, you're not even close...try seventy times seven" (Matthew 18:21–22, my paraphrase). Jesus was not putting a limit on forgiveness in this passage. He was expressing our need to be as ruthless in offering forgiveness as our Father is. Dear ones, it's easy to forgive when you understand how God has forgiven you. But many people do not understand what true forgiveness is—and what it is not. (So I'll be diving into that, in detail, in the next few chapters.)

BEING A SERVANT

The entire chapter of Luke 17 details how as Christ-followers we can learn to deal with offense. In Luke 17:7–10, Jesus taught about being a servant:

> *And which of you, having a servant plowing or tending sheep, will say to him when he has come*

in from the field, "Come at once and sit down to eat"? But will he not rather say to him, "Prepare something for my supper, and gird yourself and serve me till I have eaten and drunk, and afterward you will eat and drink"? Does he thank that servant because he did the things that were commanded him? I think not. So likewise you, when you have done all those things which you are commanded, say, "We are unprofitable servants. We have done what was our duty to do" (NKJV).

If Jesus were speaking today, He would have said, "Which of you, having an employee..." And while this may seem out-of-context with His discussion on offense, it's not. It's just the next step in our understanding of forgiveness. Forgiveness is a command from God. As His servants, we must let go of offense and release people with the same forgiveness He has given us—even if we are never thanked for it. Forgiveness isn't something extra we do to get bonus points from God. It's something He expects from us.

As ambassadors of Christ, we are here to serve others, not be served. That's the point of this example. Servants know that no one owes them a thing. They serve with zero expectation of honor, praise, recognition, or even thanks. In a way, being a servant is like being a dead person. And just like dead people cannot be offended, when we die to ourselves and take up the heart of a servant, no one can offend us.

If someone has wronged you, and you think—*They owe me! I can't forgive until they pay!*—you're the one paying. The devil is using that attitude of offense to steal the Word of God from your heart. If you let it continue, you will end up paying for that attitude in the form of sleepless nights and poisoned relationships. Don't waste your life expecting your offenders to change. Without God, they can't. Without God, we're all nothing. We have no kindness, no goodness in the flesh. Don't expect perfection from yourself or others; you will be disappointed. Only God is worthy of that expectation. *"Just as the Son of Man did not come to be served, but to serve, and to give His life a ransom for many,"* commit to serving and trust God to take care of you (Matthew 20:28 NKJV). He will never disappoint.

PRACTICE THANKSGIVING

Our next defense against offense is thanksgiving. In Luke 17:11–19, we see the story of ten lepers who came to Jesus for healing. When they cried out for mercy, Jesus gave it. He told them to show themselves to the priest. As they believed and obeyed, they were healed. Though each leper recognized the miracle he had received, only one came back to thank Jesus. Jesus was surprised. He asked, *"Were there not ten cleansed? But where are the nine?"* (Luke 17:17 NKJV). Jesus obviously expected the other nine to also return and give thanks, but only the one truly understood what he had received.

Thanksgiving and worship to God should be our natural response to His acts of mercy and grace. Grateful hearts worship God no matter what is happening around them because they understand that thanksgiving is a weapon we can use against offense. It is an act of faith.

We live in an evil, fallen world where bad things happen—to everybody. In order to avoid offense, we must learn *"in everything [to] give thanks: for this is the will of God in Christ Jesus concerning you"* (1 Thessalonians 5:18). It's not that we give God thanks *for* everything that happens. We don't thank God when someone lies to us or does something evil. It's not God's will that those things happen. But *in* every circumstance, we can find something for which to be thankful. We can give thanks for God's faithfulness in the face of human unfaithfulness. We can be thankful for His protection and provision in the midst of suffering. And we can give thanks for the victory to come.

When you fellowship with Jesus in your hurts, you bond with the Lord. We see this in human relationships as well. Two people with the same hurts bond when they fellowship together. So when we hurt, we must learn to turn to the Lord in faith. That is how supernatural healing of the soul occurs. In Philippians 3:10, Paul wanted to experience a deeper relationship with Christ. He wanted to know the Lord in *"the power of his resurrection, and the fellowship of his sufferings."* As I mentioned in a previous chapter, in this life we must suffer as Jesus suffered in some things, but in that suffering, we experience a deeper fellowship with God.

When we suffer wrongfully, Jesus understands. He's been there. And He can comfort us in it (see Hebrews 4:15). When we commit ourselves *"to him that judgeth righteously,"* God touches our emotions. And as we spend time with Him, He heals our hearts—even in the midst of suffering (1 Peter 2:23). Go to God and let the healing begin. Thank God for helping and healing you. Thank Him for loving you. Your thankfulness will slam the door to offense.

KINGDOM FOCUS

As Luke continued recording Jesus' discussion on offense, he noted:

> *Now when He was asked by the Pharisees when the kingdom of God would come, He answered them and said, "The kingdom of God does not come with observation; nor will they say, 'See here!' or 'See there!' For indeed, the kingdom of God is within you." Then He said to the disciples, "The days will come when you will desire to see one of the days of the Son of Man, and you will not see it. And they will say to you, 'Look here!' or 'Look there!' Do not go after them or follow them. For as the lightning that flashes out of one part under heaven shines to the other part under heaven, so also the Son of Man will be in His day. But first He must suffer many things and be rejected by this generation. And as it was in the days of Noah, so it will be also in the days of the Son of Man: They ate, they drank, they married wives, they were given in marriage, until the day that Noah entered the ark, and the flood came and destroyed them all.*

> —LUKE 17:20–27 NKJV

This next defense against offense is a little less obvious. Here, Jesus taught about the coming manifestation of God's kingdom. He said that the kingdom of God will come with tribulation, hardship, and suffering. Paul affirmed this in Acts when he told the disciples that *"we must through much tribulation enter into the kingdom of God"* (Acts 14:22). While God's kingdom is in us, it is not yet manifest on Earth. But Jesus is coming back. And when He does, He will inaugurate a new heaven and a new earth free of the effects of sin and Satan. Free from offense.

Jesus said that day will be like the days of Noah. People will be living their lives, distracted by natural desires, worries, and cares. They won't be focused on God's kingdom or His purposes, and they will miss His salvation. But Jesus warned His followers to be different. We should be living as if Jesus is coming back today, yet prepare as if He might not return for another ten generations. We should love people at every opportunity. Raise our families, be witnesses, make disciples, and share Christ with a lost and dying world. We should be about the Father's business—people.

Living in this way—focused on the coming kingdom—is an excellent defense against offense. Offense is a distraction from our most important work. It reorders our priorities. As believers, we are to *"seek. . .first the kingdom of God, and his righteousness; and all these things shall be added unto* [us]*"* (Matthew 6:33). We are not to seek absolution from suffering. We're not to seek retribution or revenge. We don't have time for that. Instead, we should seek first His kingdom and His righteousness. And we should trust that He will take care of everything else.

DON'T LOOK BACK

In line with this defense, we must learn to not look back. In Luke 17:28–29, Jesus said:

> *Likewise as it was also in the days of Lot: They ate, they drank, they bought, they sold, they planted, they built; but on the day that Lot went out of Sodom it rained fire and brimstone from heaven and destroyed them all* (NKJV).

This world is temporary. When Jesus returns, all those caught up in anything besides the cross will perish. That's why we must get this message out. The days of Noah and Lot foreshadow what is to come. During that time, people were so caught up in everyday life they did not prepare for the coming day of judgment. They could have joined Noah on the ark and been spared. They could have left Sodom with Lot and his family and escaped judgment.

But they were busy eating, drinking, buying, selling, and marrying. And while those things are not bad, they can distract us from the most important thing.

When Jesus returns, scripture says it will be with fire. He will execute vengeance on all those who reject the gospel. All who live in unbelief and refuse to accept God's love and salvation through Christ, as Second Thessalonians says, will perish.

> *And to you who are troubled rest with us, when the Lord Jesus shall be revealed from heaven with his mighty angels, in flaming fire taking vengeance on them that know not God, and that obey not the gospel of our Lord Jesus Christ. Who shall be punished with everlasting destruction from the presence of the Lord, and from the glory of his power; when he shall come to be glorified in his saints, and to be admired in all them that believe (because our testimony among you was believed) in that day.*
>
> —2 THESSALONIANS 1:7–10

Those who believe the gospel will be saved in that day, just as Lot and Noah were saved in their day. Until then, every person will be given the opportunity to say *yay* or *nay* to God. All will get to choose whether or not to believe (see Romans 1:20). All will choose where they wish to spend eternity. Jesus said:

> *In that day, he who is on the housetop, and his goods are in the house, let him not come down to take them away. And likewise, the one who is in the field, let him not turn back. Remember Lot's wife. Whoever seeks to save his life will lose it, and whoever loses his life will preserve it.*
>
> —LUKE 17:31–33 NKJV

Lot looked forward and was saved. But his wife refused to let go of her life in Sodom and fell under God's righteous judgment. She looked back and was destroyed (see Genesis 19:26). Had she released the life she'd known in Sodom, she would have found a new life—one of abundance and God's blessings.

I'm always amazed when someone vividly recalls the bad things that happened to them twenty years ago. They can describe details of that moment flawlessly, but cannot remember the good that's happened since. No matter how traumatic something is that happened to you or how bad something is that you have done, your healing and deliverance is not in looking back and rehearsing the event but in focusing on living well today. Jesus taught us to look forward, not back. Looking back is how offense overcomes us, but we can overcome offense by looking forward.

> *Brethren, I do not count myself to have apprehended; but one thing I do, forgetting those things which are behind and reaching forward to those things which are ahead, I press toward the goal for the prize of the upward call of God in Christ Jesus.*
>
> —PHILIPPIANS 3:13–14 NKJV

Paul had done some horrible things like holding the coats of those who stoned Stephen (Acts 7:58). Then during his ministry, he had some horrific things done to him such as being stoned and left for dead (2 Corinthians 11:25). The key to his wholeness was in pressing forward, not looking back.

As believers, we must forget the past, reach toward those things just ahead of us, and press toward our ultimate future—the prize of His calling (see Romans 8:29). All of this boils down to one simple truth: You cannot reach your destiny if you are hanging on to your past. Don't allow your past to defile your present or sabotage your future. Choose not to look back. Look forward. Press on. The prize awaits.

TRUST GOD'S JUDGMENT

Another of our defenses against offense is learning to trust in God's righteous judgment. While God does call us to make judgments about some things in this life, others are above our pay grade.

> *I tell you, in that night there will be two men in one bed: the one will be taken and the other will be left. Two women will be grinding together: the one will be taken and the other left. Two men will be in the field: the one will be taken and the other left.*
>
> —LUKE 17:34–36 NKJV

We need to be discerning (which is just another way of saying "using righteous judgment") when it comes to judging our own hearts and life. We need to judge where we work, whom we choose to marry, and how we raise our children. We need to judge our hearts in areas of thinking that we've allowed to be influenced by the world, as well as many other things in life. But judging other people, especially their hearts and motivations, is above our pay grade.

We don't get to judge who goes to heaven and who doesn't. That's God's job. We must simply trust His judgment. Romans 12:19 says, *"Dear friends, never take revenge. Leave that to the righteous anger of God. For the Scriptures say, 'I will take revenge; I will pay them back,' says the Lord"* (NLT). The passage goes on to say, *"Instead, 'If your enemies are hungry, feed them. If they are thirsty, give them something to drink. In doing this, you will heap burning coals of shame on their heads'"* (Romans 12:20 NLT). We can trust God to judge righteously. He will take care of things—in this life and the life to come.

I avoid offense as much as possible. But when I can't, when somebody does me wrong and it hurts my heart, I continue doing good and trust God to both heal my heart and judge between us. All these defenses—trusting God to judge righteously, staying focused on God's kingdom, looking toward the future, practicing thanksgiving, being a servant, and choosing forgiveness—will guard my heart from offense.

Proverbs 4:23 says, *"Keep thy heart with all diligence; for out of it are the issues of life."* The Hebrew word translated as *keep* in this verse literally means "to guard."[6] The word translated *issues* means "boundaries or borders."[7] To guard our hearts, we must be conscious of the seeds sown in them and diligent over what we choose to nurture there. The devil is constantly trying to sow the weed of offense in our hearts. But God is constantly sowing the seed of His Word. Both seeds will affect us and influence the boundaries of our lives. By guarding our hearts from offense and learning to forgive quickly, we allow the good seed of the Word to expand our borders and produce good fruit.

After Jesus' resurrection, Mary Magdalene was the first person to see the Lord's empty tomb. But she didn't understand what she saw. She wept, thinking someone had stolen Jesus' body. As Mary turned to leave the tomb, she saw someone she assumed to be the gardener (which tells me the man must have been dressed as a gardener) and asked if he knew where Jesus' body had been taken. The man called Mary by name, and everything changed. She recognized His voice and knew it was Jesus (see John 10:27; 20:15–17).

I love this picture of Jesus the gardener. It reminds me of the first man, Adam. He, too, was a gardener, a gardener of the first creation. And though Adam failed in his duty and slung that garden into chaos, Jesus, the second man and last Adam, did not fail His mission. He became the gardener of the new creation—you and me. Now Jesus is spreading His glory, through us, to a lost and hurting world (see 1 Corinthians 15:20–23, 45). That's why I don't want offense in my heart. Unforgiveness, bitterness, and offense defile me. They hinder my ability to carry Jesus' glory to the world. And while I must guard my heart diligently, I'm not alone in this work. Jesus, the gardener of my heart, is an expert at pulling weeds!

CHAPTER SEVEN

RELEASING OFFENSE

And be kind to one another,
tenderhearted, forgiving one another,
even as God in Christ forgave you.
—EPHESIANS 4:32 NKJV

Part of spiritual maturity is learning to correctly process offense, which as we've seen, starts with a good defense. Recognizing the root cause of offense helps us stop giving Satan space to steal our peace or destroy our relationships. In time, and with practice, we may even stop getting offended at all! Impossible, you say? No, it's not. If it were impossible to live life without offense, God wouldn't have given us Psalm 119:165: *"Great peace have they which love thy law: and nothing shall offend them."* It is possible to not get offended. That doesn't mean you and I will not have opportunities to get offended, but by guarding our hearts we can learn to live free from offense.

Of all the tools God gave us to defend against offense, forgiveness is both the most powerful and least understood. Many people believe biblical forgiveness to be something it is not. They find it difficult to extend forgiveness to unrepentant people. And in some cases, because of the pain and loss associated with certain circumstances, they believe forgiveness to be unattainable. Often, these people confuse forgiveness with trust, or they think because they still feel pain over a situation they haven't forgiven. But forgiveness is not as hard as you may think. It's simply an extension of God's love toward us and an overflow of that love toward others.

In First Corinthians 5, Paul invoked church discipline on a man who was sleeping with his stepmother. Of course, we all know that sleeping with a stepmother is wrong; no good can come from it. But in this instance, the man was not repentant. Paul warned the church that if his sin was left unresolved it would be like leaven spreading through the whole assembly. Eventually that sin would destroy them (see 1 Corinthians 5:6–7). Paul was clear in his instructions to the church that the purpose of the man's discipline was to bring repentance. Though the church was bragging about their love toward this man in

Releasing Offense

sin, it was not love to allow sin and the consequences of sin to harm him or the church.

Hebrews talks about this connection between love and chastening. God loves us as we are, but He also loves us too much to allow us to stay in sin. So He lovingly chastens us. Not out of wrath or anger, but out of love (see Hebrews 12:6). That's what Paul wanted for the church at Corinth.

Thankfully, the church listened to Paul and gave us a beautiful example of appropriate church discipline. The discipline they invoked led the man to godly repentance, and in Second Corinthians, Paul wrote to encourage the church to forgive the man and restore him to fellowship:

> Sufficient to such a man is this punishment, which was inflicted of many. So that contrariwise ye ought rather to forgive him, and comfort him, lest perhaps such a one should be swallowed up with overmuch sorrow.
>
> —2 CORINTHIANS 2:6–7

I cannot stress enough how important it is to understand that the church did not discipline this man out of vengeance or ill will. They disciplined him out of love— love for God, the man, and the church at large. Jesus said, in John 14:23, *"If anyone loves Me, he will keep My word..."* (NKJV). He went on to make a profound statement in verse 24. *"He who does not love Me does not keep My words..."* (NKJV). In other words, our obedience to God's Word is in direct proportion to our love for God. Jesus repeated this in John 15:10 when He said, *"If you keep My commandments, you abide in My love, just as I have kept My Father's commandments and abide in His love"* (NKJV).

Jesus also told us to love our neighbor as ourselves (see Matthew 22:39). But what many people don't realize is that in this instance Jesus was quoting from Leviticus 19:17–18, which says:

> *You shall not hate your brother in your heart. You shall surely rebuke your neighbor, and not bear sin because of him. You shall not take vengeance, nor bear any grudge against the children of your people, but you shall love your neighbor as yourself; I am the Lord* (NKJV).

It is a form of hate to not confront the sin that is destroying someone's life. It's a form of hate to take vengeance on them or hold onto offense. To truly love our neighbor, as God loves, we must warn them of the deadliness of sin. But we must also forgive.

Now no chastening seems to be joyful for the present, but painful; nevertheless, afterward it yields the peaceable fruit of righteousness to those who have been trained by it. Therefore strengthen the hands which hang down, and the feeble knees, and make straight paths for your feet, so that what is lame may not be dislocated, but rather be healed. Pursue peace with all people, and holiness, without which no one will see the Lord: looking carefully lest anyone fall short of the grace of God; lest any root of bitterness springing up cause trouble, and by this many become defiled.

—HEBREWS 12:11–15 NKJV

What a sobering thought! Bitterness and unforgiveness is a poison. It's the only poison we drink convincing ourselves that it will kill someone else. And it's not just something unbelievers or baby Christians deal with. This verse in Hebrews is written to Jewish Christians filled with the Holy Spirit. In it the writer says, "Look, if you don't yield to the grace of God and let forgiveness permeate your heart, you will fall short of His grace. A root of bitterness will spring up inside of you and cause you and many others to be defiled" (my paraphrase).

Like living in habitual, unrepented sin, unforgiveness corrupts our souls. When we choose not to forgive, we yield to demonic influence and give Satan the opportunity to steal, kill, and destroy our lives (see John 10:10). That's why Paul wrote to urge the Corinthians to forgive their brother in Christ and restore him to fellowship.

> *Therefore I urge you to reaffirm your love to him. For to this end I also wrote, that I might put you to the test, whether you are obedient in all things. Now whom you forgive anything, I also forgive. For if indeed I have forgiven anything, I have forgiven that one for your sakes in the presence of Christ, lest Satan should take advantage of us; for we are not ignorant of his devices.*
>
> —2 CORINTHIANS 2:8–11 NKJV

Nobody wakes up one day with a root of bitterness in his or her heart. Bitterness comes from not processing offense and choosing to not forgive. Each is a bait of Satan. Taking that bait turns us into a full-course meal for the enemy to devour. If you remember, offense starts when we nurse a wrong done to us. As we rehearse it, it morphs into unforgiveness, and a seed of bitterness takes root in our hearts. When we allow bitterness to grow, we cut God off from reversing the offense and healing our hearts. Instead, we begin dispersing it to everyone around us and cause others to become offended. Like leaven spreading though bread dough, our unprocessed offense will spread through an entire community and defile it. Harboring unforgiveness leads to fruitlessness. We become barren like Saul's daughter, Michal. Though we try to seek God and do the right thing, we don't see results. But there is hope. We can become fruitful again.

The cure to fruitlessness is repentance and forgiveness. Unfortunately, both have been misunderstood and incorrectly taught in the Church for decades. Our God is a merciful and gracious God. When we fail, He does not cut us out of fellowship. He offers forgiveness (see 1 John 1:9). It's so important to repent when we fail and receive forgiveness from God, because a major part of forgiving others is receiving our own forgiveness. God has forgiven us of so much. It empowers us to forgive others when we understand how forgiven we are.

However, many choose not to forgive because they don't know what forgiveness is. They may desire to obey scripture, but they simply don't know how. Others have a misconception of what forgiveness looks like and don't believe they can forgive. A clear understanding of scripture can release both of these people to forgive. But before we dive into what biblical forgiveness is, let's look at what it is not. Forgiveness is not:

1. EMOTIONAL

Forgiveness is not an emotion. Many people feel locked into unforgiveness because their emotions have been damaged. They incorrectly believe that they haven't truly forgiven when they still feel emotional pain over an incident.

Dear ones, sometimes the things people choose to do cause pain. And often, that pain takes time and the intervention of God to heal. But that doesn't mean we can't choose to forgive. Years ago, my father crushed me deeply. His actions hurt me so badly I fell to the ground and cried in deep sorrow. As horrible as I felt, I chose to forgive my dad—without him asking—but I still carried the pain and brokenness of what he did to me and my family for a long time. If I measured forgiveness by my emotional pain, I would have trapped myself in unforgiveness and might not be in ministry today. I forgave my father. Not for his sake, but for my sake and the sake of the kingdom.

Forgiveness is a choice. When you choose to forgive, the door to your heart opens and allows God to heal your emotions. Unforgiveness keeps the emotional wound open. Forgiveness closes it. Had I not been able to separate my pain from forgiveness, I might have missed the beauty of my father's repentance. And my father did repent, years later. By that time, I had no unforgiveness or pain left in my heart to deal with. God had healed me.

2. FORGETTING

Forgiveness does not equal forgetting. How could I tell someone going through an unwanted divorce that they haven't really forgiven their mate until they no longer remember the wrong done to them? Yet I've heard people preach, "You haven't forgiven until you forget." That is wrong, and quite frankly, cruel. I can't imagine anything worse to say to someone who has experienced child molestation or some other form of abuse. It is impossible to forget that kind of thing. And in some cases, it's actually healthy not to forget. If your uncle molested you as a child and has not repented, I recommend you remember that. You don't want to put your own children in the same position you were in.

Though people may mean well when they say this, there is no such thing as religious amnesia. If this adage were true, then the Jewish people would never have been able to forgive the Germans. How could anyone forget what Hitler and the Nazis did? I think this misconception comes from Philippians 3:13–14, which says:

> *Brethren, I do not count myself to have appre-hended; but one thing I do, forgetting those things which are behind and reaching forward to those things which are ahead, I press toward the goal for the prize of the upward call of God in Christ Jesus* (NJKV).

Paul's *forgetting* here is not a state of memory loss. Paul didn't forget Stephen's stoning. How could he? He held the coats of those who threw the stones. Paul remembered his persecution of the church. He gave his testimony countless times throughout his ministry (see 1 Corinthians 15:9). Paul fully recalled hauling Christians out of their homes, imprisoning them, and beating them in the synagogues. So what did he mean when he wrote about forgetting? Paul's forgetting in this passage is actually forgiveness—and in his case, self-forgiveness.

True biblical forgiveness is not allowing the past to define the present or sabotage our future. When God forgave me, I started over as a man without a past (see 2 Corinthians 5:17). God doesn't hold my past against me, so why should I hold it over myself? Like Paul, I have chosen to forget, which means I do not allow my past to prophesy my future. Now when I look back, I only see the redemptive work of Christ. I don't think, talk, or act out of my past failures. I remember what God has done, and I think, talk, and act out of the good He has wrought. I let go of what is behind me and conform myself to the image of God's dear Son, trusting Him to bring good out of my life—no matter what is in my past (see Romans 8:28).

3. TRUST

Forgiveness is not trust. It is possible to forgive someone and not trust them. (In certain circumstances, it's actually wisdom.) Trust, by definition, must be earned. Forgiveness is a gift.

We control when and whom we choose to forgive. The burden of trust rests in the hands of the person asking for it. If someone has had an affair, his or her spouse may forgive, but that doesn't mean the spouse won't struggle with trust. Even if the unfaithful spouse is truly repentant, it takes time to rebuild what was broken. What if I, as a pastor, discovered that someone in my church had a history of pedophilia? I would certainly forgive that person, but I'm not going to trust him or her to serve in children's church. Everyone understands that. A former pedophile isn't trustworthy in that area. I can still love that person enough to help him or her. But I will walk in wisdom and wait to extend trust.

We should not trust those who are untrustworthy. Scripture is very clear (see 1 Thessalonians 5:12; 1 Timothy 3:1–7; 2 Timothy 2:2). Even God, who has forgiven us all fully, does not release certain treasures of His kingdom to untrustworthy people. Instead, He follows this principle:

> *He who is faithful in what is least is faithful also in much; and he who is unjust in what is least is unjust also in much. Therefore if you have not been faithful in the unrighteous mammon, who will commit to your trust the true riches?*
>
> —LUKE 16:10–11 NKJV

Faithful here means trustworthy.[8] How we handle a small thing like mammon or money is connected to God's ability to trust us with true riches. If we can't handle money and the temptations that come with finances, how will we handle spiritual gifts and authority? How can God trust us to steward the hearts of His people? God's forgiveness is not conditional, but trust is.

4. RECONCILIATION

Reconciliation is not the same thing as forgiveness. Forgiveness is my choice. Reconciliation involves other people, and in some instances, is simply not possible. You and I can't control other people. We can't make decisions for them or force them to do what is necessary to rebuild trust. If the other party in our offense doesn't want to reconcile or isn't willing to change his or her lifestyle, we can't make that happen. Does that mean we can't forgive? No. While I forgive freely as a gift, restoration involves repentance on the other's part. As a believer who has experienced God's forgiveness, I forgive people whether they repent or not. But I can only reconcile with them when there is a change of mind and direction.

If you're in business with a man who runs off with the secretary and all the money, you're going to have to forgive him. You're going to have to release the past so it doesn't dictate your future—even if his actions caused you to go bankrupt. Whether that person comes back to you in repentance or not, you must extend mercy, love, and grace to him. (However, I don't recommend you go into business with him again.) But there's nothing you can do if the other person doesn't want to reconcile. Forgiveness is on you. It's your responsibility. Trust and reconciliation is on him.

5. IGNORING OFFENSE

Forgiveness is also not ignoring an offense. Lots of Christians ignore offense hoping it will go away. But this just leaves the matter unresolved. Offense doesn't disappear simply because you don't pay attention to it. People may say, "Time heals all wounds," but there are some things time can't heal. Only God can. Only God can heal, cleanse, and restore the brokenhearted (see Psalm 147:3). And He can only do that when we choose to forgive.

While we can let go of imaginary or accidental offenses, (that's how *"love covers a multitude of sins"* [1 Peter 4:8 NLT]), overlooking actual offense is not love or forgiveness. Ignoring a problem won't heal it. Actual offense requires a resolution (see Matthew 18:15). I know. It seems easier to avoid the conflict. But by not dealing with it, we actually harbor offense in our hearts.

I've had to confront people to deal with offense, both in my personal life and in ministry. And I'm sure you will, too. By "confronting," I'm not talking about being mean or accusatory. I'm talking about kindly and humbly going to a brother and saying, "I am struggling with something. This offended me, and we need to talk about it." Dealing with offense can be hard, but we can't suppress those hurts and expect them to go away. We have to release the offense and choose to forgive.

Now that you know what forgiveness is not, I hope you find that choosing to act on forgiveness (which I talk about in the next chapter) becomes easier.

CHAPTER EIGHT

BIBLICAL FORGIVENESS

*Give us this day our daily bread, and forgive
us our debts as we forgive our debtors.*
—MATTHEW 6:11–12 NKJV

So, what is *biblical* forgiveness? A quick New Testament search of Jesus' teachings will give you the simplest definition. *Forgiveness* is a "releasing of debt." Have you ever heard someone say, "You owe me an apology?" Maybe you've even said this yourself. But true forgiveness says, "You don't owe me a thing."

I did not understand this concept of releasing debt early in my Christian life. When someone wronged me, I felt that it was just and right for them to repent and apologize to me. To not demand that felt unjust. I didn't understand that releasing them from debt was actually releasing me from the deadly force of unforgiveness.

By holding on to unforgiveness, I tie myself to the hurt that person's actions caused. But when I forgive—when I release the debt—I sever that tie. I release myself from that event so I can heal and move on with life. In forgiveness, I am released from the prison of my past to enjoy the freedom of my future. What that person did cannot harm me any longer.

It is not our place to make people pay for the wrong done to us. If you're waiting for someone to apologize before you forgive, you may be waiting a long time. By locking yourself into unforgiveness like that, you allow it to turn into a root of bitterness that will poison you and others. Eventually that bitterness will hinder your effectiveness in the kingdom of God. As believers, we are called to love and forgive as we have been forgiven (see Ephesians 4:32).

In Luke 7, Jesus went to eat at a Pharisee's house. While He was eating, a woman entered the house and approached Him. She began to weep and wash Jesus' feet with her tears, drying them with her hair. The Pharisee was offended. He couldn't understand why Jesus would extend grace to the town harlot.

As the woman washed Jesus' feet, He began to teach. He told a parable of two debtors who owed someone money. One debtor owed 50 denarii. The other owed 500.

(In New Testament times, a denarii was about a day's wage.[9] Today, that would be like owing a little less than two months wage, around $7,000–8,000, verses owing nearly a year-and-a-half's wage, or $77,000.[10]) But the creditor forgave them both. "Which of them will love him more?" Jesus asked.

"I suppose the one whom he forgave more," the Pharisee answered.

Jesus replied, *"Therefore I say to you, her sins, which are many, are forgiven, for she loved much. But to whom little is forgiven, the same loves little"* (Luke 7:36–47 NKJV).

When we understand how completely God has forgiven us, we are willing to love generously. Unfortunately, most Christians don't know how much they've been forgiven. They have forgotten what life was like before knowing Christ. They've forgotten how unrighteous they once were, so they only love a little. They are like that Pharisee. They never smoked or drank. They never cussed or hung around those who did. They think their sin isn't as bad as everyone else's so there isn't much for Jesus to forgive. But self-righteousness and pride are hideous evils in God's sight.

It doesn't matter who you are or where you come from—before Jesus, your sins were many. Mine were, too. All of us owed God a debt we could never pay. And

Jesus forgave it. Every one of us should love as extravagantly as the woman in Luke 7, because we have been forgiven much!

When Jesus taught us how to pray, He even highlighted the importance of forgiving as we have been forgiven. *"And forgive us our debts, as we forgive our debtors"* (Matthew 6:12 NKJV). And each time Jesus taught about forgiveness, He explained it in terms of releasing debt. As I mentioned earlier, when Peter asked, *"Lord, how often shall my brother sin against me, and I forgive him? Up to seven times?" Jesus' response shocked him. "I do not say to you, up to seven times, but up to seventy times seven"* (Matthew 18:21–22 NKJV). Maybe Peter was expecting a pat on the back for being so "generous" with his forgiveness. But Jesus wasn't impressed. He told Peter to forgive 490 times—in one day! I don't know if even the most hardhearted person on the planet can sin that often against one person in a single day. But I also don't think Jesus was trying to quantify forgiveness with this response. He was just saying that forgiveness should be limitless.

As impossible as forgiving those who have wronged you seems, you can forgive anybody of anything if you understand that, in simplicity, forgiveness is releasing someone of debt. Jesus went on to illustrate His point with a story:

Therefore the kingdom of heaven is like a certain king who wanted to settle accounts with his servants. And when he had begun to settle accounts, one was brought to him who owed him ten thousand talents. But as he was not able to pay, his master commanded that he be sold, with his wife and children and all that he had, and that payment be made.

—MATTHEW 18:23–25 NKJV

You're in pretty bad debt when your life can't cover it. When your wife, children, and all your possessions get sold to pay a debt, you know it's serious.

The servant therefore fell down before him, saying, "Master, have patience with me, and I will pay you all." Then the master of that servant was moved with compassion, released him, and forgave him the debt. But that servant went out and found one of his fellow servants who owed him a hundred denarii; and he laid hands on him and took him by the throat, saying, "Pay me what you owe!" So his fellow servant fell down at his feet and begged him, saying, "Have patience with me, and I will pay you all." And he would not, but went and threw him into prison till he should pay the debt. So when his fellow servants saw what had been done, they were very grieved, and came and told their master all that had been done. Then his master, after he had called him, said to him, "You wicked servant! I forgave you all that debt because you begged me. Should you not also have had compassion on your fellow servant, just as I had pity on you?" And his master was angry, and delivered him to the torturers until he should pay all that was due to him. So My heavenly Father also will do to you if each of you, from his heart, does not forgive his brother his trespasses.

—MATTHEW 18:26–35 NKJV

This whole story is a reflection of the heavenly Father. God has forgiven us a great sin debt—one so large that even if He'd patiently waited our entire lives, as the master in this story, we'd never be able to balance our account. Jesus paid our debt through His suffering and death on the cross. He released us of any obligation we owed the Father and offered forgiveness to the whole world. Now, as in the parable, our Master expects that those of us who have received His forgiveness offer it to our fellow debtors.

May we not be like the servant who refused to forgive. In Jesus' story, the master was furious that his unforgiving servant would be so caviler with what he received. The master took the man by the throat and imprisoned him. Dear ones, that's exactly what we do when we withhold forgiveness and demand that others apologize to us and repay what they owe. And worse? We tell others about what that person did to us and disperse our offense throughout a community. This greatly displeases God.

In Jesus' parables on forgiveness, He never said we would "feel like" forgiving others. He did not say we had to forget what was done to us or immediately restore that person to trust and fellowship. Neither did He say we should just ignore what was done. When we release someone from debt, we are not excusing what they did or saying that there won't be any consequences for those actions. We are simply releasing them to God. And if they do not repent, they will reap their own harvest—but not at our hands.

Through forgiveness, we release others of debt to us and transfer their judgment into God's hands. They will answer for what they did, but not to us. They will have to settle accounts with God—if not in this life, then in the life to come. God's judgment is righteous. He sees the motivations of every heart. He sees the extenuating circumstances. And He is long-suffering. It may seem as if people are getting away with sin, but that doesn't mean there is no justice. When we are wronged, the wisest thing we can do is to let it go and trust God to handle it in righteousness. Then, once we cut the ties of unforgiveness, we are free to be healed.

CHOOSING PEACE

One element of Jesus' story that people struggle with is that when we who have been forgiven don't forgive, we are given over to tormentors (see Matthew 18:34). Some people discount this part completely, saying, "How could a loving God torment anyone?" Others debate over who (or what) the tormentors are. I've seen small wars break out over these things. Some people are convinced the tormentors are demons. Others aren't sure if a Christian can have a demon. They think perhaps it's pain or worldly people reacting to our hypocrisy. Others are sure it's governmental authorities. On and on the debate escalates, sometimes to the point of foolishness. But these people miss the point. If we refuse to forgive, we are turned over to tormentors. Period. Tormentors torment. It doesn't matter if the source is the devil, the pain of your past, your own conscience, or something else.

Most people who are tormented are totally confused. They think the source of their torment is what others have done to them. They say, "Of course I'm tormented. I was molested as a child." Or, "Of course I'm tormented. My wife ran off with somebody else." Or, "If you only knew what they did to me." And I respond with, "If you only knew what they did to me, you would understand that forgiveness is possible." We've all experienced things that at the time seem unforgiveable.

Look at Stephen. He was stoned for preaching the gospel. And yet, as he lay dying, he forgave those who were stoning him.

> *And they stoned Stephen as he was calling on God and saying, "Lord Jesus, receive my spirit." Then he knelt down and cried out with a loud voice, "Lord, do not charge them with this sin." And when he had said this, he fell asleep.*
>
> —ACTS 7:59–60 NKJV

That's amazing. Notice again what Stephen said. "Lord, do not charge them with this sin." Stephen followed Jesus' example by releasing the debt, knowing that he was releasing the people who killed him to God's righteous judgment (see Luke 23:34). And even in the midst of physical torture, he felt no emotional torment.

Dear ones, if you hold on to your pain, if you hold on to a perceived right to be upset and demand repayment of wrong, you're going to live in the torment of that wrong forever. In Jesus' story of the ungrateful servant, He never said that the offense you experienced was the cause of torment. He said that unforgiveness was the cause of torment. While this truth may shock you, it is actually good news. If the source of your torment were what people did to you, there would be no hope of escaping it. However, if the source of your torment is your own unforgiveness, you can change that instantly. Just choose to forgive and release others from debt.

In simplicity, *unforgiveness* is holding onto offense and charging people for their sin—sometimes with interest. *Forgiveness* is choosing to live like Christ and release people of their debt—even when they truly owe you. Ephesians 4:32 says, *"And be ye kind one to another, tenderhearted, forgiving one another, even as God for Christ's sake hath forgiven you."* Forgiving others starts with receiving forgiveness from God then extending that forgiveness to others. As we honor the Lord in forgiveness, we are released from torment so that God can heal our hearts of hurt and brokenness. We win by forgiving!

Though our emotions may struggle with a sense of injustice as we take these first steps toward living free of offense, we can trust that God will honor His Word as we walk in obedience to it. Forgiveness is incredibly worthwhile. It:

- Releases people from debt to us and transfers them to God's righteous judgment.
- Releases us from torment.
- Releases healing to our hearts.
- Protects us from bitterness.
- Delivers us from offense.
- Reverses Satan's strategies against us.
- Keeps us from becoming defiled and unfruitful.
- Demonstrates God's love to others.

We know that we will experience trials and tribulations in this world, and that if we let them, those trials will produce offense. But as the world grows ever darker, we are called to shine bright *"in the midst of a crooked and perverse generation"* (Philippians 2:15 NKJV). We are called to forgive. Forgiveness embraces both God's mercy and grace. *Mercy* is not getting the consequences of what we deserve. *Grace* is getting the good we don't deserve. When others wrong us, they don't deserve forgiveness.

But neither did we. Yet God extended mercy. How can we do any less?

Understanding these simple truths changes everything. By the grace of God, we can combat this culture of offense and stop Satan in his tracks by simply choosing to live free of offense. We can join in God's work of grace by rising above our hurt and spreading His love and forgiveness to each person in our lives. And we can teach our children, neighbors, and friends to navigate a world filled with offense.

That's why it is so important for us to know God's Word and develop relationships with people who will hold us lovingly accountable to the truth. But we can't do that if we are overcome with offense. And while it's impossible to avoid every situation that tempts us to be offended, we can uproot offense before it takes root in our hearts and produces death. Choose to forgive. Choose to heal. It will free you from the trap of offense and transform your life from the inside out.

CHAPTER NINE

BEING AND STAYING HEALED

The Lord is near to those who have a broken heart, and saves such as have a contrite spirit.
—PSALM 34:18 NKJV

Just as offense has a process that can lead to bitterness and a prison of torment, so does healing. While some people are healed instantly and perfectly, most people have a healing journey experience. Once an offense is forgiven and released, the healing journey begins. Any deep wound or hurt can and will be healed as we come to Jesus. He is near to us when we come to Him in and with our hurt and bruised hearts. His love is everlasting and unconditional.

When broken, many experience a sense of rejection from family and peers because they may not be the easiest to be around when they are hurting. In their distress and pain, they may say and do things that are not a true reflection of who they are. An otherwise good-natured dog cannot be trusted when wounded. Now I'm not saying that we are all wounded dogs; however, I have watched wounded and hurt people act out in ways they would normally be appalled by. The good news is that even when we experience rejection from other people, God will never cast us aside, no matter how broken we may feel.

Isaiah the prophet addresses God's willingness to heal our hurts and His commitment to never cast us off in our brokenness:

GOD'S LOVE AND PATIENCE

Behold! My Servant whom I uphold, My Elect One in whom My soul delights! I have put My Spirit upon Him; He will bring forth justice to the Gentiles….A bruised reed He will not break, and smoking flax He will not quench; He will bring forth justice for truth.

—ISAIAH 42:1–3 NKJV

This is a direct reference to Jesus, the Elect of God. He is the great healer of hearts. We must learn to behold Him and look to Him instead of focusing on our hurts. Earnestly observing who God is and what He has done for us—instead of focusing on people and what they have done to us—will speed up our healing process. God put His Spirit upon Jesus to bring about justice, which involves healing us from the pain caused by the works of Satan. In Luke 4:18, Jesus declared who He is and His purpose on earth:

> *The Spirit of the Lord is upon Me, because He has anointed Me to preach the gospel to the poor; He has sent Me to heal the brokenhearted, to proclaim liberty to the captives and recovery of sight to the blind, to set at liberty those who are oppressed* (NKJV).

The imagery used in the Hebrew text of Isaiah 42:3—*"A bruised reed He will not break, and smoking flax He will not quench"*—describes God's true compassion for hurting people and His willingness to care for them. Young Hebrew children would gather reeds from the riverbanks and make musical instruments from them. Many of the reeds the children harvested would be damaged and bruised and, therefore, would be tossed aside as worthless.

God does not consider us worthless or useless at all. Our lives are to be musical instruments for the praise and glory of God's goodness. However, many times when we get bruised and broken, people tend to consider us as damaged goods and useless. God never casts us aside, regardless of the brokenness we have experienced. Jesus heals and restores us to be that praise unto His glory.

The "smoking flax" reaffirms this truth. When the oil ran out of the lanterns, the wick would smolder and stink up the house. The occupant of the home would take that wick and throw it out the window to spare the home from the unpleasant odor of the smoking flax.

Broken and hurting people can be a challenge to be around because of the negative overflow of their brokenness. God is patient though, and when we come to Him and allow Him to heal us, He is faithful to refill our lanterns with fresh oil. He then relights our lanterns to allow that sweet fragrance of His knowledge to flow through us: *"Now thanks be to God who always leads us in triumph in Christ, and through us diffuses the fragrance of His knowledge in every place"* (2 Corinthians 2:14 NKJV).

How amazing is that! God promises to always lead us in triumph and, in that, cause us to emit a beautiful fragrance of His glory and goodness. When we come to Him in faith-filled obedience, laying our hurts and offenses before Him, He transitions us from a "smoking flax" to a "scented candle," filling our immediate orbit with praise and thanksgiving. Thanks be to Jesus, *the* healer of a broken heart.

Luke 4:18-19 declares that Jesus was anointed to *"heal the brokenhearted"* and *"set at liberty them that are bruised."* To *bruise* means to crush.[11] *Broken* means to crush completely, to shatter, be bruised.[12] *Hearted* refers to the thoughts or feelings, the mind (soul), the middle.[13] Your soul is in the middle between your spirit and body. It is the part of you that can agree with your spirit (spiritually minded) or your body (carnally minded).

Romans 8:6 speaks of the value of being spiritually minded: *"For to be carnally minded is death, but to be spiritually minded is life and peace"* (NKJV). Obviously, this does not refer to just having our feelings hurt, being oversensitive, or just touchy, touchy about things. The brokenhearted are those who have been deeply crushed and bruised, like for instance, through the loss of a child or an unwanted divorce.

This is what happened to my mother when my brother was killed in an automobile accident as a teenager. The loss of her son crushed her to the point that it was all she focused on, and ultimately, it caused my parent's marriage to dissolve, and they divorced. They did not know how to process their hurt and turn to the Lord and allow Him to heal them. Though my mother did give her heart to the Lord at the end of her life, she never recovered from the brokenness caused by my brother's death and the unwanted divorce that took place soon after that.

I too was broken when this happened. I actually cried so hard that I passed out. I had never experienced a hurt that deep and crushing before or since. I saw my life descend into all the symptoms and pain of a broken heart. I was a broken vessel unable to contain any good thing, being a broken reed and a smoking flax. However, in May of 1980, I had an encounter with Jesus. I saw an open vision of the Cross and what took place there on my behalf. The first thing Jesus did in this encounter was to heal my broken heart.

Remember that Isaiah 42:1 encourages us to *"Behold my Servant."* We can be healed of our brokenness when we behold Jesus. To *behold* means to be held by, to gaze upon. When we turn our hearts toward Jesus, He delights in healing us and making us whole again: *"He heals the brokenhearted and binds up their wounds"* (Psalm 147:3 NKJV). The Holy Spirit healed me and bound up the wound of my emotional pain so I could now contain the good things of God in my life.

RECEIVING HEALING

Faith comes by hearing and hearing by the Word of God (see Romans 10:17). These scriptures on healing will produce faith in our hearts to come and receive from the Lord. He heals our hearts and binds up our wounds. When we allow this process of healing and binding to happen in our lives, we will then become a blessing to others, because we can now contain and retain the things of the kingdom of God.

Broken vessels leak right? God wants to heal that brokenness and then fill us with joy and thanksgiving. Unresolved offenses keep us bound and often in torment. Unforgiveness will lock us into a prison and leave us bound by chains of hurt and pain. Forgiveness releases us from that prison. Being healed by Jesus is like a spiritual jail break.

Jesus' mission was to heal and liberate: *"God anointed Jesus of Nazareth with the Holy Spirit and with power, who went about doing good and healing all who were oppressed by the devil, for God was with Him"* (Acts 10:38 NKJV). (This sounds a lot like Isaiah 61:1 and Luke 14:18–19.) The gospel message is clear that God anointed and sent Jesus to heal and do good.

Through His death, burial, and resurrection, Jesus executed judgment on Satan's works. All healing of our hearts and bodies is God's vengeance on the works of the devil. God delights in healing us and reversing the works of Satan. Jesus is alive and well today, living in and through His followers, and He is still anointed to heal and do good, executing judgment and vengeance on the works of the devil.

GOD'S COMFORT

It is also God's will to comfort:

> ...*To comfort all who mourn, to console those who mourn in Zion, to give them beauty for ashes, the oil of joy for mourning, the garment of praise for the spirit of heaviness; that they may be called trees of righteousness, the planting of the Lord, that He may be glorified.*
>
> —ISAIAH 61:2–3 NKJV

Zion is a reference to the Church (see Hebrews 12:22–23), those who have made Jesus Lord and Savior, those who have their names registered in Heaven. In other words, if you have been born again, this verse is talking about you. God desires to comfort, not condemn you; to receive, not reject you; to draw nigh, not cast you out. He wants to take the ashes in your life created by hurt, pain, and brokenness and bring beauty from them. If you are in a state of brokenness while reading this, it may be hard to receive or even conceive of such good news. But I encourage you to give God your broken heart and allow Him to turn it around for you. Watch Him break you out of the prison of hurt and bondage and give you a garment of praise. Have faith and trust Him, for He is most trustworthy.

Trust His love and compassion for you and His desire to turn things around for you. Only He can take the ashes of a dysfunctional life and turn them into a beautiful garden of blessings and fruitfulness. Only He can replace mourning with the oil of joy, replace your heaviness with a garment of praise. This is exactly what Jesus did for me in 1980, and He can do it for you. As Peter the apostle said, *"In truth I perceive that God shows no partiality"* (Acts 10:34 NKJV).

> *Blessed be the God and Father of our Lord Jesus Christ, the Father of mercies and God of all comfort, who comforts us in all our tribulations that we may be able to comfort those who are in any trouble, with which we ourselves are comforted by God.*
>
> —2 CORINTHIANS 1:3–4 NKJV

God is the God of all comfort and healing. He comforts us when tribulation brings brokenness of heart. But He doesn't stop there. Through His comfort and healing in our lives, He enables us to be conduits of His comfort and healing to others.

The apostle Peter is an example of this powerful truth. When Jesus and His disciples were in the Garden of Gethsemane, Jesus knew Judas was about to betray Him. Jesus also knew the weakness of people, even His own disciples, and He prophesied what God had revealed to Him from scripture about His disciples:

> *All ye shall be offended because of me this night: for it is written, I will smite the shepherd, and the sheep of the flock shall be scattered abroad. But after I am risen again, I will go before you into Galilee.*
>
> —MATTHEW 26:31–32

Peter vehemently protested this, saying, *"Though all men shall be offended because of thee, yet will I never be offended"* (Matthew 26:33). Peter was convinced that, because of his love for Jesus, he would never take offense. He acknowledged the weakness of others—"though all men shall be offended"—but he defended his own loyalty and commitment to the master—"I will never be offended."

In the following verses of Matthew 26, Jesus confronted Peter personally and proclaimed that before daybreak the next day, Peter would deny Him three times (see Matthew 26:34). Unwisely, Peter doubled down on his defense of his faithfulness, loyalty, and commitment, declaring: *"Though I should die with thee, yet will I not deny thee. Likewise also said **all** the disciples"* (Matthew 26:35). Peter wasn't the only one who rejected what Jesus said. All of the disciples thought they were beyond offense and were committed to Him unto death. This passage shows us how important it is to believe God's Word above our own feelings and opinions. It also reveals how we cannot put any confidence in our flesh. We are all weak independent of God and must rely on Him completely. None of us are beyond being offended or failing and falling. We must all be humble, seeing our need for God in all things.

Jesus told them they would all be offended, and they were, even when they said they wouldn't be. Jesus told them they would forsake Him and scatter, which they did. On the night of His betrayal, all of the disciples scattered, and Peter denied Him three times before daybreak. Everything happened just as Jesus had said it would happen.

Luke 22 records another account of this same event and gives us further insight into what took place:

> *And the Lord said, "Simon, Simon! Indeed, Satan has asked for you, that he may sift you as wheat. But I have prayed for you, that your faith should*

not fail; and when you have returned to Me, strengthen your brethren."

But he said to Him, "Lord, I am ready to go with You, both to prison and to death."

Then He said, "I tell you, Peter, the rooster shall not crow this day before you will deny three times that you know Me."

—LUKE 22:31–34 NKJV

Jesus knew that Satan was personally targeting Peter in order to take him out, but Jesus said He would pray for Peter. I have often read this and thought, *I need more than prayer; do something!* But it's important to pay attention to what Jesus prayed—that Peter's faith would not fail. Jesus prays this for us as well. He prays that regardless of the opposition, trial, persecution, or affliction we may face, our faith will not fail to keep us focused on Him, understanding that the challenges we experience are the trying of our faith. Such experiences happen to all of us in this life, but our faith determines whether these experiences will take us out or make us stronger. This is why Jesus prays for our faith. Satan desires to hurt and offend us, hoping that we will separate from Jesus, but Jesus prays that we will stand strong in Him (see Romans 8:35–39).

Jesus knew that Peter would fail—as we all do when operating in our own strength—but Jesus also knew that the faith residing in Peter would not fail. Jesus prayed that Peter's faith would enable him to endure the trial of Jesus' death. Once Peter had returned to Jesus, he would then be able to strengthen his brothers in Christ (see Luke 22:32). Peter felt crushed and brokenhearted when the rooster crowed and he realized he had denied the Lord, just as Jesus said he would. He had failed, but he repented, and in that repentance, he was converted. The Holy Spirit comforted him, and he then became a vessel of that comfort to the other believers. He was able to comfort others with the same comfort he had received. Though he had personally failed, his faith prevailed, just as Jesus prayed it would. The ashes of that failure were turned to beauty that has benefited the entire body of Christ.

After the resurrection Jesus asked Peter three times if he loved Him:

> *So when they had eaten breakfast, Jesus said to Simon Peter, "Simon, son of Jonah, do you love Me more than these?"*
>
> *He said to Him, "Yes, Lord; You know that I love you."*

He said to him, "Feed My lambs."

He said to him again a second time, "Simon, son of Jonah, do you love Me?"

He said to Him, "Yes, Lord; You know that I love You."

He said to Him, "Tend My sheep."

He said to him the third time, "Simon, son of Jonah, do you love Me?"

Peter was grieved because He said to him the third time, "Do you love Me?" And he said to Him, "Lord, You know all things; You know that I love You."

Jesus said to Him, "Feed My sheep."

—JOHN 21:15–17 NKJV

This story gives us three important keys about Peter's restoration after his failure. First, Peter had obviously learned his lesson; he now realized that Jesus does know all things. He was not nearly as confident in himself, but had greater confidence in Jesus' words. Second, Jesus *publicly* asked Peter about his love three times because He knows the power of words for life or death (see Proverbs 18:21). Peter had spoken words of death, denying the Lord, in public, so those words needed to be countered and canceled out by public words of life—Peter's public confession of his love and commitment to Jesus. In this way, Jesus healed the brokenness of Peter's heart. Third, Jesus tells Peter a very specific way to demonstrate his love for Jesus—feeding the lambs and sheep by teaching them God's love for them. (In this passage, *lambs* refers to immature Christians and *sheep* refers to the mature.) After he had received comfort and healing, he was called to transmit that comfort and healing to others. Peter's faith had prevailed, and as a result, his life and teachings have strengthened the body of Christ for centuries.

Jesus desires to heal your heart of all hurts and offenses, and He often uses a combination of comfort and instruction from the Holy Spirit, the scriptures, and other people (the body of Christ).

THE HOLY SPIRIT

About the Holy Spirit, Jesus said, *"And I will pray the Father, and he shall give you another Comforter, that he may abide with you forever"* (John 14:16). Healing in our hearts involves receiving comfort (see Isaiah 40:1–5; 61:1–6), and one of the many assignments of the Holy Spirit is to comfort us. This is the same Spirit who was upon Jesus, anointing Him to heal the brokenhearted. And Jesus promised, *"I will not leave you comfortless: I will come to you*"(John 14:18). Through the Holy Spirit, Jesus comes to us and continues to heal broken hearts today.

In Acts 9:31, we read that the churches received the comfort of the Holy Spirit after a season of persecution. He brought healing and wholeness of heart in the midst of their tribulations, and that is what caused the early Church to multiply and grow.

That is how I have grown, too. In May of 1980, as I mentioned previously, I had a vision of the Cross, saw my identification with Christ, and received healing in my heart from the Holy Spirit. Prior to that, I had lived a totally dysfunctional life because of my grief and pain over the death of my brother. But when the Holy Spirit revealed Christ and the Cross to me, I experienced wholeness. I experienced the gospel, and wholeness was the result. I saw Jesus' death, burial, resurrection, and ascension into heaven where He is seated on the throne. I saw myself in Him in that journey—my identification with Christ unto salvation. The power of that vision was supernatural, and it transformed me. This is one of the most significant ways in which we receive healing in our hearts—through the comfort of the Holy Spirit.

My life changed from ashes to beauty, from heaviness and oppression to praise, from mourning to dancing. The Holy Spirit recovered all the "desolate land" in my heart created by brokenness in my life. I experienced restoration of all that Satan had stolen and entered into the wholehearted life in Christ. But it didn't stop there. I also developed a deep hunger for the Bible and began to experience healing and comfort in my heart through the scriptures. While the Holy Spirit brought a healing and wholeness to my heart; it was the scriptures that strengthened my heart.

THE SCRIPTURE

The second way we receive healing in our hearts and maintain our healing is through reading the scripture. As I read in the scriptures that God *"sent his word and healed them, and delivered them from their destructions"* (Psalm 107:20), that He is the one *"who redeems your life from destruction, who crowns you with loving kindness and tender mercies"* (Psalm 103:4 NKJV), I began to experience the reality of that healing in my life. I was able to walk and live in my healing by the faith that came from scripture.

God uses both the Holy Spirit and His Word to deliver us from our destructions. The destructive force of unresolved hurt and pain is healed through the power of God's Word, which is like medicine to the soul and cleansing to the body. Jesus referenced this healing quality of the Word when He said, "*Sanctify them by Your truth. Your word is truth*" (John 17:17 NKJV). The truth supernaturally sanctifies us, which means it "sets us apart." God's Word, as truth, has the power to heal and cleanse us, and that is why it should be the final authority in our lives.

The truth of scripture, illuminated to our hearts by the Spirit, brings freedom from any prison of past hurt or brokenness (see John 8:31–32). Satan, the father of lies, entraps us in prisons of pain and suffering through lying to us about our identity based on our past. He tells us things like, "You're not worthy of God's love or blessings." "You're flawed, an exception to God's plan of wholeness and prosperity." "You are just damaged goods, unusable and disqualified from God's best for your life." These three lies in particular kept me in bondage and defeat for the first 15 years of my Christian life. However, in May of 1980 the vision of the cross brought a healing of my feelings and emotions (past hurts and pains) and the scriptures renewed my thoughts to now walk in the fulness of the healing (Romans 12:2).

I'm convinced that had I not renewed my mind (thoughts) to my new identity I saw in the vision, I would have eventually been hurt again and returned to brokenness and defeat. This is what happens to so many good Christian people. God will touch them by the Spirit bringing freedom and healing, but He desires to equip us through His word to walk and live in that freedom. Satan steals the healing because of a lack of knowledge (Hosea 4:6, 3 John 2). The Holy Spirit and Word agree and work together in our lives. We need both. It was God's word confirming what I saw in the vision that gave me the faith to stand and overcome any lies of Satan trying to rob me of my victory. I discovered my true identity in Christ, and through it, I found healing in my soul (my thoughts). The Holy Spirit broke me out of the prison of pain and hurt then it was the Word that kept me from going back.

The Word is like a mirror of the Spirit world; it reveals new creation realities in our spirits. Through the Word, I saw who I was in Christ because of the finished work of the Cross. God's truth exposed all the lies and set me free from their bondage, and that understanding brought great healing and wholeness in my life (see 2 Corinthians 5:17; Ephesians 4:24). When we hear, see, and renew our minds to what Jesus has done in our born-again spirits through the Cross, we will experience supernatural transformation and healing for our broken hearts.

The Bible tells us we will face afflictions, and those afflictions can damage our hearts. But God *"is near to those who have a broken heart, and saves such as have a* contrite spirit" (Psalm 34:18 NKJV). God promises that when we face afflictions, He will deliver us *"out of them all"* (Psalm 34:19 NKJV). We face many hurts and much brokenness in this fallen world, but we have the assurance of God's comfort and healing in every affliction. Through His Spirit, through His Word, and through other people, God is the healer of our hearts.

OTHER PEOPLE

One of the great miracles of God's healing power in our lives is that we then get to become vehicles of His healing for other people. We are the body of Christ in the earth and Jesus is the head of the body. Christ lives in us, *"the hope of glory"* (Colossians 1:27). Jesus lives in and works through His body, the church. We all need each other in the challenges of this life. I have had things happen to me over the years that could have broken me and bruised me. God has used so many different members of His body to comfort and encourage me in God's love for me. The Holy Spirit and living word is in His body and He uses us to be a blessing to one another. What an honor and privilege to see God work in us and through us healing broken hearts around us.

Just like God restored Peter and sent him to strengthen his brothers, He is restoring us to now go and strengthen our brothers and sisters. Be bold and courageous in sharing Jesus—the healer of broken hearts. Freely we have received, now we need to freely give. In Acts 1:8 Jesus said, *"...you shall receive power when the Holy Spirit has come upon you..."* The same Spirit that was on Jesus to heal the broken hearted is on His body, the church to minister healing. The same power that was on Jesus to heal sickness and disease and to do good (Acts 10:38), in on His body, the church, you and me. Receive God's healing and now become a vessel of His goodness to others who are broken.

For our lives to prosper, we must maintain a good and whole heart. God has given us three primary ways to receive healing: through the Holy Spirit, through scripture, and through other people. I've experienced healing of my heart through all three of these avenues and prospered as a result. If we let Him, Jesus wants to use all three of these to bring wholeness to our hearts and lives.

WALKING IN OUR HEALING

He prays for you, like He did for Peter, that in the hard moments, your faith will not fail. You have a part to play. Jesus does not simply rescue you but empowers you to overcome and to live in His kingdom perspective. On the journey of receiving healing for a broken heart and learning to live free of offense, you must engage with these five simple steps:

1. GIVE YOUR LIFE TO THE LORD.

If you have made Jesus the Lord of your life, then the Spirit of God lives inside you to comfort and guide you. If you have not yet made Jesus Lord of your life, it is as simple as this:

> *If you confess with your mouth the Lord Jesus and believe in your heart that God has raised Him from the dead, you will be saved. For with the heart one believes unto righteousness, and with the mouth confession is made unto salvation.*

> ROMANS 10:9–10 NKJV

2. FORGIVE OTHERS AND YOURSELF.

In the process of healing the heart, forgiving yourself is as important as forgiving others. Remember, forgiveness is an act of your will, not a feeling or emotion, as we discussed in depth in Chapter 8. Jesus told us to pray, *"And forgive us our sins, for we also forgive everyone who is indebted to us..."* (Luke 11:4 NKJV). Forgiveness is an essential part of the new covenant life and walking in freedom and victory.

3. RENEW YOUR MIND TO GOD'S WORD AND PROMISES.

Spending time with Jesus, learning from Him and studying His Word, will help you keep your heart and mind focused on the things of God, not on your circumstances. This is an important key in being able to release offense and live in peace. As Paul wrote, *"And do not be conformed to this world, but be transformed by the renewing of your mind, that you may prove what is that good and acceptable and perfect will of God"* (Romans 12:2 NKJV).

4. GUARD YOUR HEART.

Understand this: Offense is a deadly tactic that Satan uses to try to kill, steal, and destroy your life. Keeping your heart full of the Holy Spirit and God's Word will powerfully protect your heart against this tactic. Proverbs 4:23 warns: *"Keep your heart with all diligence, for out of it spring the issues of life"* (NKJV). To keep your heart free from hurt, pain, and offense, you must diligently guard it and proactively pursue the things of God. Jesus told us that the words we say betray the condition of our hearts. He conveyed this message in Matthew 12:34 during one of His teachings where He said, *"... For out of the abundance of the heart the mouth speaks."* In other words, you can judge the condition of your heart by listening to what is coming out of your mouth. Are words of life, joy, and peace flowing out of you, or are your words full of murmuring and complaining? If it is the later, you can find freedom by coming to Jesus and filling your heart with His Word.

5. TESTIFY OF YOUR HEALING (SHARE WITH OTHERS).

Revelation 12:11, *"And they overcame him by the blood of the Lamb, and by the word of their testimony; and they loved not their lives unto the death."* Philemon 1:6, *"that the communication of thy faith may become effectual by the acknowledging of every good thing which is in you in Christ Jesus."* When we share what Jesus does in our lives our faith become effectusal. It strengthens our faith and resolve. Tell others what Jesus has done and is doing in your life.

CONCLUSION

Isaiah 61:3-7 declares all the blessings and benefits of our healing and wholeness of heart. In poetic language he paints a life of God's good plan for us and generations to come. Isaiah 61:3 says that we will be *"...trees of righteousness, the planting of the Lord, that He may be glorified."* We will be firmly planted and mature becoming a place of refuge for the hurting all around us. He heals, comforts, and restores us to be vessels of healing and restoration to others. Isaiah 61:4 says, *"And they shall rebuild the old ruins, they shall raise up the former desolations, and they shall repair the ruined cities, the desolation of many generations."* Many of the hurts and brokenness we experience come from previous generations. Many times, the pains and hurts our parents experience and the ashes created by their brokenness become generational.

Poverty, alcohol, drug abuse, sexual abuse, and many other forms of brokenness become generational. Your heling stops the generational pain and brokenness. IT can all stop with your healing and forgiveness and now generation blessing can start with you as well.

Isaiah 61:6-7, *"But you shall be named the priest of the Lord, they shall call you the servants of our God. You shall eat the riches of the Gentiles and in their glory you shall boast. Instead of your shame you shall have double honor."* Wow! We are now named priests of God and His servants, no longer identified by our hurts and pains. All the shame from our brokenness is replaced with honor from God. What a wonderful reversal from victim to victory stature. The head now and not the tail.

The journey of healing of our hearts is not always an easy one, but it is one of utmost importance. Jesus paid the price to free us from a life of offense and brokenness, so don't settle for anything less. Come to Him and give Him your sins, hurts, pains, and brokenness. Receive His healing rays of love and compassion. Watch Him bless you and generations after you.

NOTES

1. Blue Letter Bible, s.v. "Skandalon" (Strong's G4625); https://www.blueletterbible.org/lexicon/g462 5/kjv/tr/0-1/.

2. Ibid., s.v. "Krin" (Strong's G2919); https://www.blueletterbible.org/lexicon/g2919/csb/mgnt/0-1/.

3. Ibid., s.v. "Aske" (Strong's G778); https://www.blueletterbible.org/lexicon/g778/kjv/tr/0-1/.

4. Ibid., s.v. "Agape" (Strong's G26); https://www.blueletterbible.org/lexicon/g26/kjv/tr/0-1/.

5. Ibid., s.v. "Ouai" (Strong's G3759); https://www.blueletterbible.org/lexicon/g3759/kjv/tr/0-1/.

6. Ibid., s.v. "Nar" (Strong'Es H5341); https://www.blueletterbible.org/lexicon/h5341/kjv/wlc/0-1/.

7. Ibid., s.v. "Tô'ô" (Strong's H8444); https://www.blueletterbible.org/lexicon/h8444/kjv/wlc/0-1/.

8. Ibid., s.v. "Pistos" (Strong's G4103); https://www.blueletterbible.org/lexicon/g4103/kjv/tr/0-1/.

9. *Full Life Bible Commentary of the New Testament*, French Arrington and Roger Stronstad, editors (Grand Rapids, MI: Zondervan, 1999).

10. Based on average the American salary in 2020 of $56,000/year, as found at https://www.census.gov/library/publications/2021/demo/p60-273.html.

11. Blue Letter Bible, s.v. "Thraus" (Strong's G2352); https://www.blueletterbible.org/lexicon/g2352/kjv/tr/0-1/.

12. Ibid., s.v. "Suntribo" (Strong's G4937); https://www.blueletterbible.org/lexicon/g4937/kjv/tr/0-1/.

13. Ibid., s.v. "Kardia" (Strong's G2588); https://www.blueletterbible.org/lexicon/g2588/kjv/tr/0-1/.

ABOUT THE AUTHOR

Duane Sheriff is the Founding Pastor and Senior Elder of Victory Life Church, a multi-campus church headquartered in Durant, Oklahoma. Duane travels the world speaking at conferences and churches, and he is a frequent teacher at Charis Bible College. His television ministry also broadcasts on various stations. He loves helping people discover their identity in Christ and experience transformation through the Word of God. Duane released his first book, *Identity Theft,* in 2017. Since then, he has authored three more books: *Our Union with Christ, Better Together,* and *Counterculture.* Duane and his wife, Sue, have been married since 1980 and together have four children and eleven grandchildren.

DSM

DUANE SHERIFF MINISTRIES

We exist to help people grow in Christ.
Since 1983 we have been promoting the Word
of God, and helping people develop a personal
relationship with Jesus.

Learn more at
www.pastorduane.com

From
DUANE SHERIFF

God has called YOU to be an agent of cultural change!

America is experiencing a cultural revolution. Against the onslaught of conflicting political agendas, powerful media pressures, and radical ideologies, what should Christians think? How should we respond?

In *Counterculture,* Pastor Duane Sheriff reveals how the "woke" movement has a form of godliness but denies the power of the cross. Instead of aligning with the dominant cultural trends, believers must rise up and forge a Kingdom culture, countering critical race theory with "critical grace theory"—the truth and power of the gospel.

God has called you as an agent of change! And change happens one heart at a time, one good deed at a time, and one vote at a time. Begin now!

Purchase your copy wherever books are sold

From
DUANE SHERIFF

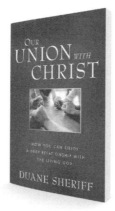

God loves you incredibly, faithfully, and with a kind of love that is beyond compare. In fact, God wants you to so thoroughly understand and be encompassed by His love that He gave you a picture of it!

God reveals this picture in the God-ordained covenant of marriage. While *Our Union with Christ* is not a typical book on marriage, it reveals the relationship Jesus has with His Church. The apostle Paul speaks of the marriage relationship between a husband and wife and Christ and the Church in Ephesians 5 and refers to it as a "great mystery."

Author and pastor Duane Sheriff shares this epic love story and revelation that will illuminate your union with Jesus. These truths will establish and secure you in God's eternal love and abiding care, and you will never again doubt God's goodness toward you. As you come to know by the Spirit the great mystery, you will grow in intimacy with the Lord, your faith will soar, and you will experience the peace of God like never before.

Purchase your copy wherever books are sold

From
DUANE SHERIFF

With so many obstacles arrayed against them, how can any couple hope to make it in today's world?

Health issues. Financial pressures. Misunderstandings. Sexual broken-ness. Societal confusion. As if these storms aren't bad enough, Satan is specifically targeting Christian marriages.

When the winds howl and the rains fall, it is vital for every marriage to be secured against the tempests of life with strong anchor lines that keep your relationship thriving.

In *Better Together,* Pastor Duane Sheriff offers six trustworthy anchors to steady your marriage through inevitable storms. Plus, each chapter includes focused questions and action steps to help you live out these marital truths in reflective, intentional ways!

Marriage is an incredible gift when God is central to the relationship. And *Better Together* will deepen your understanding of godly principles that enable you to experience the oneness and strength God intends for your relationship!

Purchase your copy wherever books are sold

Equipping Believers to Walk in the Abundant Life
John 10:10b

Connect with us on

Facebook @ **HarrisonHousePublishers**

and Instagram @ **HarrisonHousePublishing**

so you can stay up to date with news

about our books and our authors.

Visit us at **www.harrisonhouse.com**